Gallery of Hope & Joy

ADAM OTOKITI

Gallery of Hope & Joy

Curated by
Adam Otokiti

Published by Think Beyond Boundaries Press
1569 Solano Avenue, #544
Berkeley, CA 94707
thinkbeyondboundaries.com

ISBN: 09860912-2-7
ISBN -13: 978-0-9860912-2-3

Printed in USA
2017 First Edition

ACKNOWLEDGMENTS

The following writers and artists are exhibited in the Gallery of Hope & Joy:

Robert Browning, Marvell, Cottle, Campbell, Beauchene, Sir H. Davy, Leonard Bacon, Pope, Spenser, Milton, Robert C. Winthrop, Phillips Brooks, William Winter, Bishop King, Walter Scott, Bishop Berkely, Cottager and Artisan, J. Beaumont, Demosthenes, Massinger, Maltbie Babcock, Plautus, Oliver Wendell Holmes, Krishna, Glanvill, Dean Stanley, George D. Prentice, Nat. Lee, John Ruskin, Beecher, Julia C. R. Dorr, Johnson, Sunday School Times, Bulwer-Lytton, Maturin, Ben Jonson, Caravaggio, Botticelli, Charles Willson Peale, Degas, Toulouse-Lautrec, Rembrandt, Trumbull, Hogarth, Rivera, Delacroix, Picasso, Benozzo Gozzoli, Titian, Blume, Klee, Dali, Jan Van Eyck, Bruegel the Elder, Edward Hicks, Magdalen Master, Seurat, El Greco, Whistler, David, Turner, Benozzo Gozzoli, Gerome, Botticelli, Bruegel the Elder, Henri Rousseau, Rivera, Chardin, and Kokoschka.

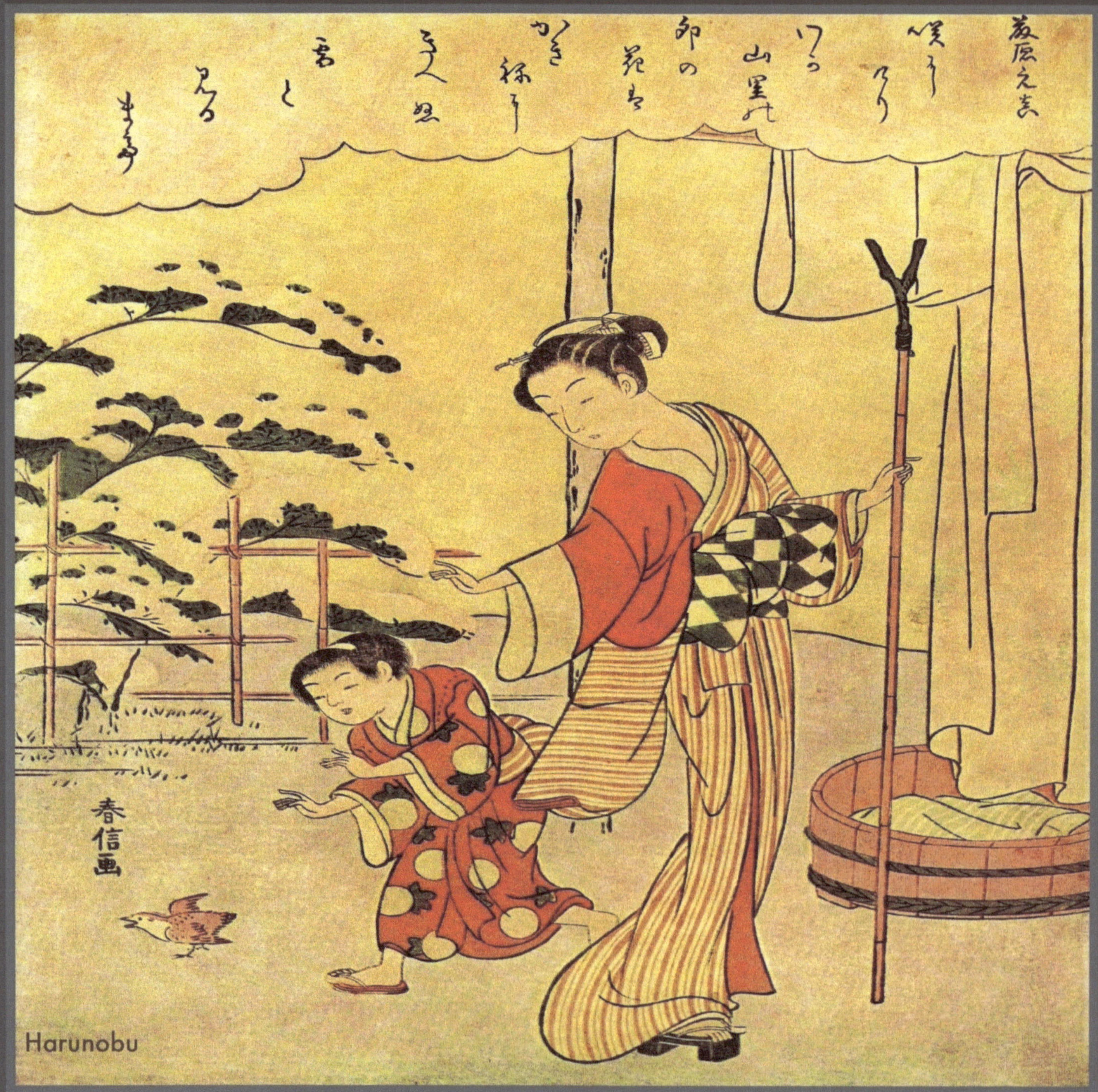
春信画
Harunobu

A REFLECTION

The Past is memory,
the insight to life.
The Present is real,
the joy of living.
The Future is imagination,
the hope of being alive.

— A. Otokiti

Life is what we are alive to. It is not length, but breadth. To be alive only to appetite, pleasure, pride, money-making, and not to goodness and kindness, purity and love, history, poetry, music, flowers, stars, God and eternal hopes, it is to be all but dead.

— Maltbie Babcock

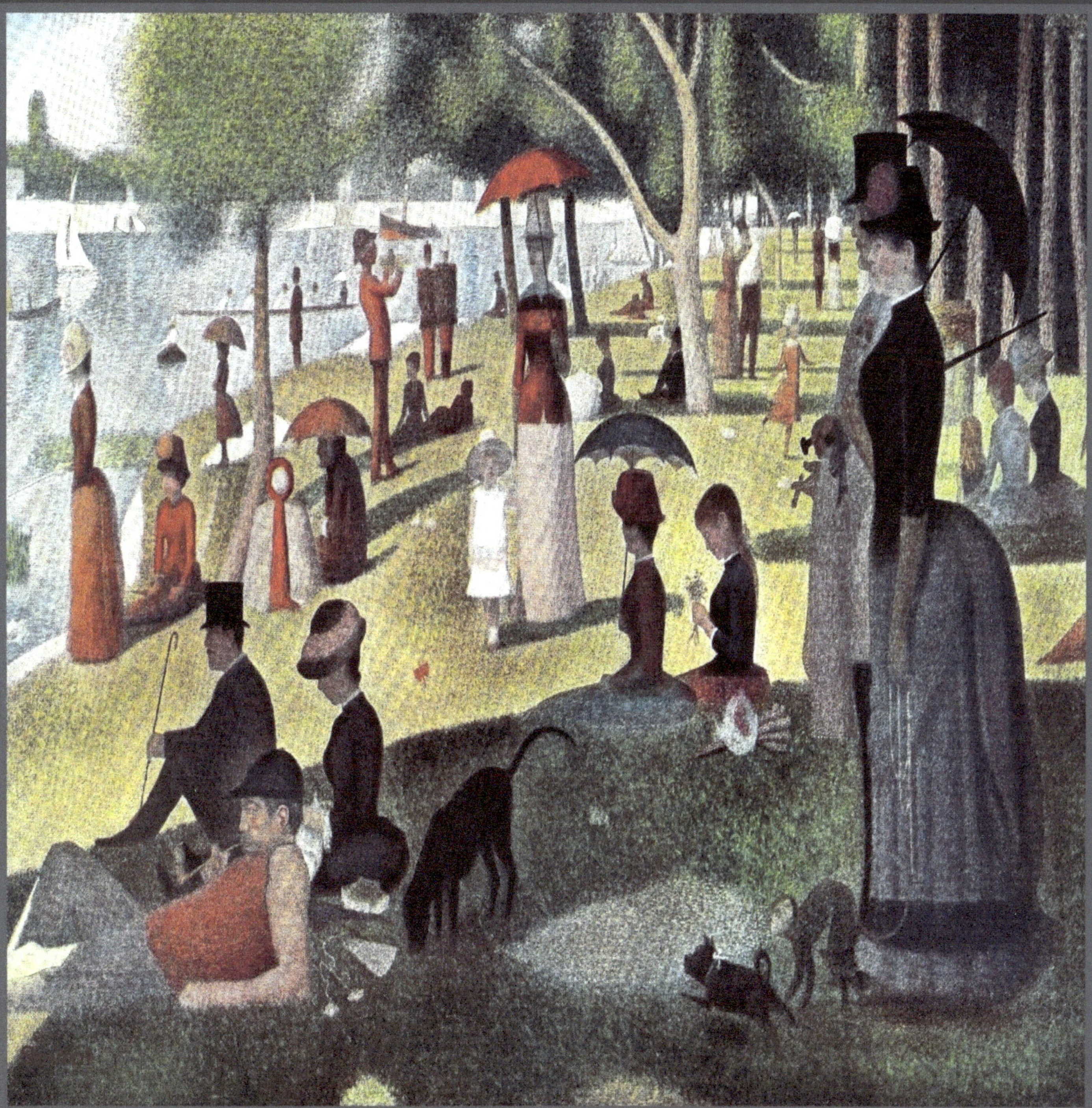

Every one of us knows how painful it is to be called by malicious names, to have his character undermined by false insinuations, to be overreached in a bargain, to be neglected by those who rise in life, to be thrust on one side by those who have stronger wills and stouter hearts. Everyone knows, also, the pleasure of receiving a kind look, a warm greeting, a hand held out to help in distress, a difficulty solved, a higher hope revealed for this world or the next. By that pain and by that pleasure let us judge what we should do to others.

— Dean Stanley

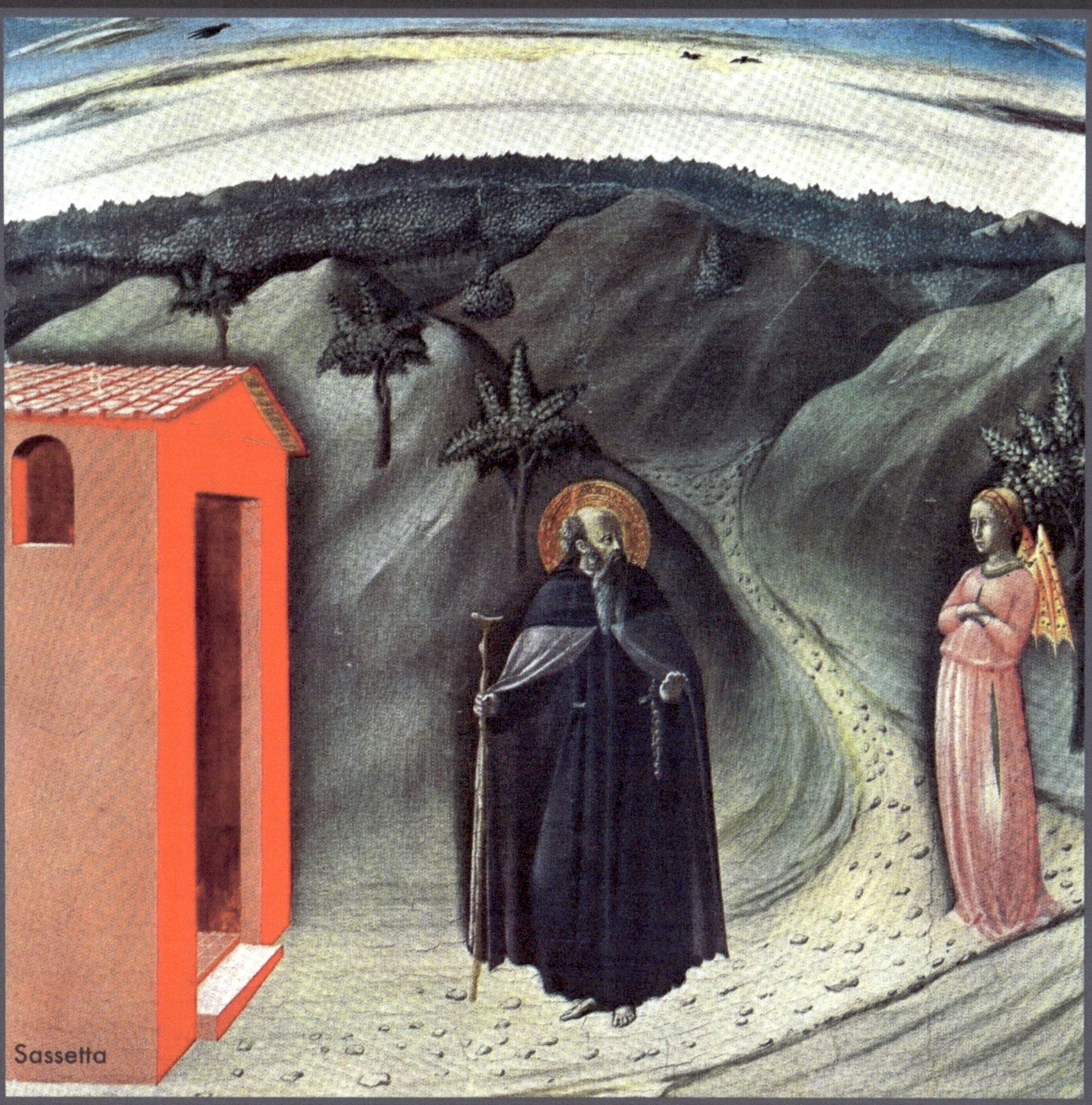
Sassetta

Love, hope, fear, faith —
these make humanity;
These are its sign and note
and character.

— Robert Browning

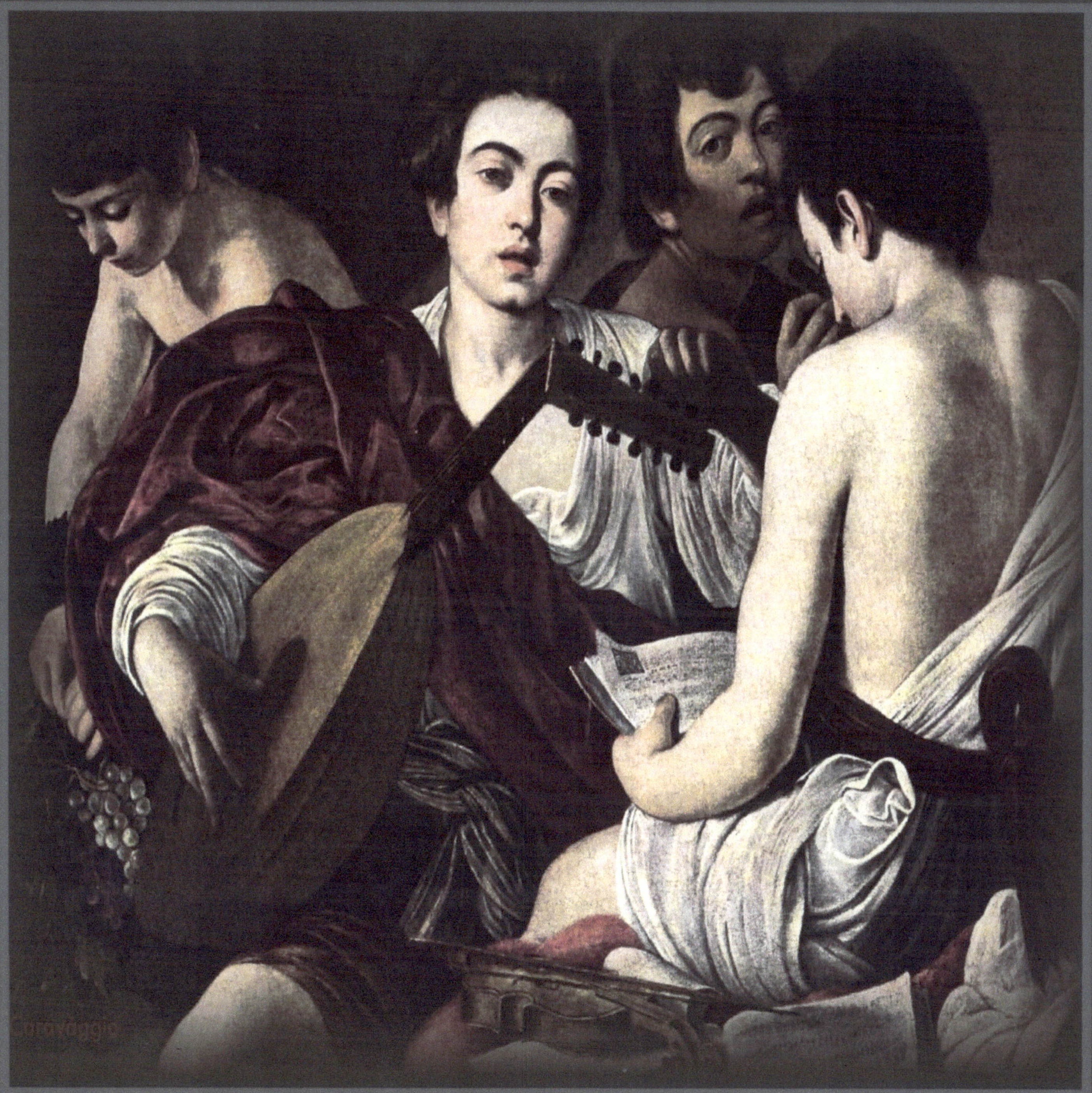
Caravaggio

Though I carry always
some ill-nature about me, yet
it is, I hope, no more than
is in this world necessary for a preservative.

— Marvell

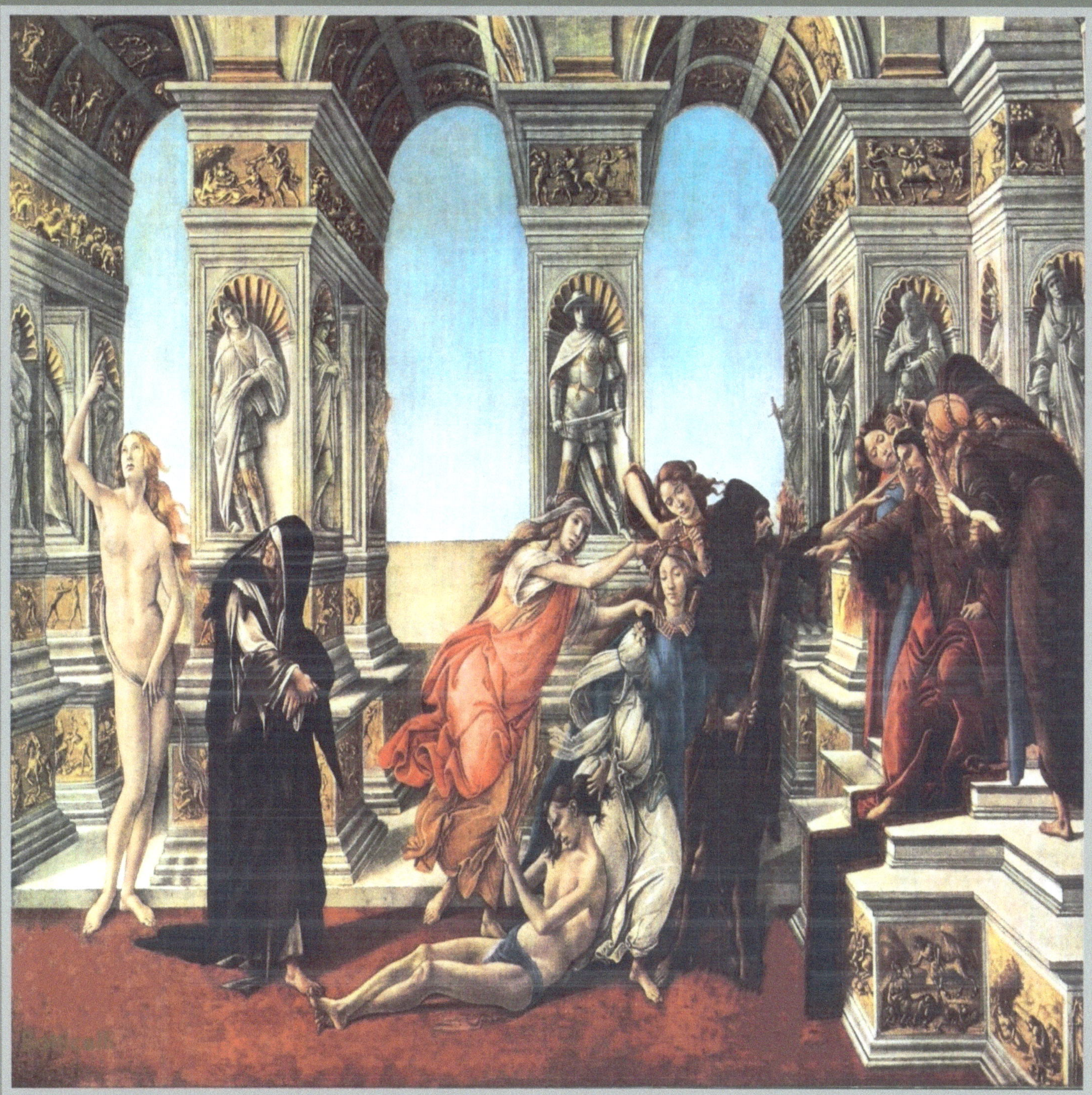

Joy thou bring'st, but mix'd
with trembling; Anxious hopes
and tender fears, Pleasing hopes
and mingled sorrows, Smiles of
transport dashed with tears.

—Cottle

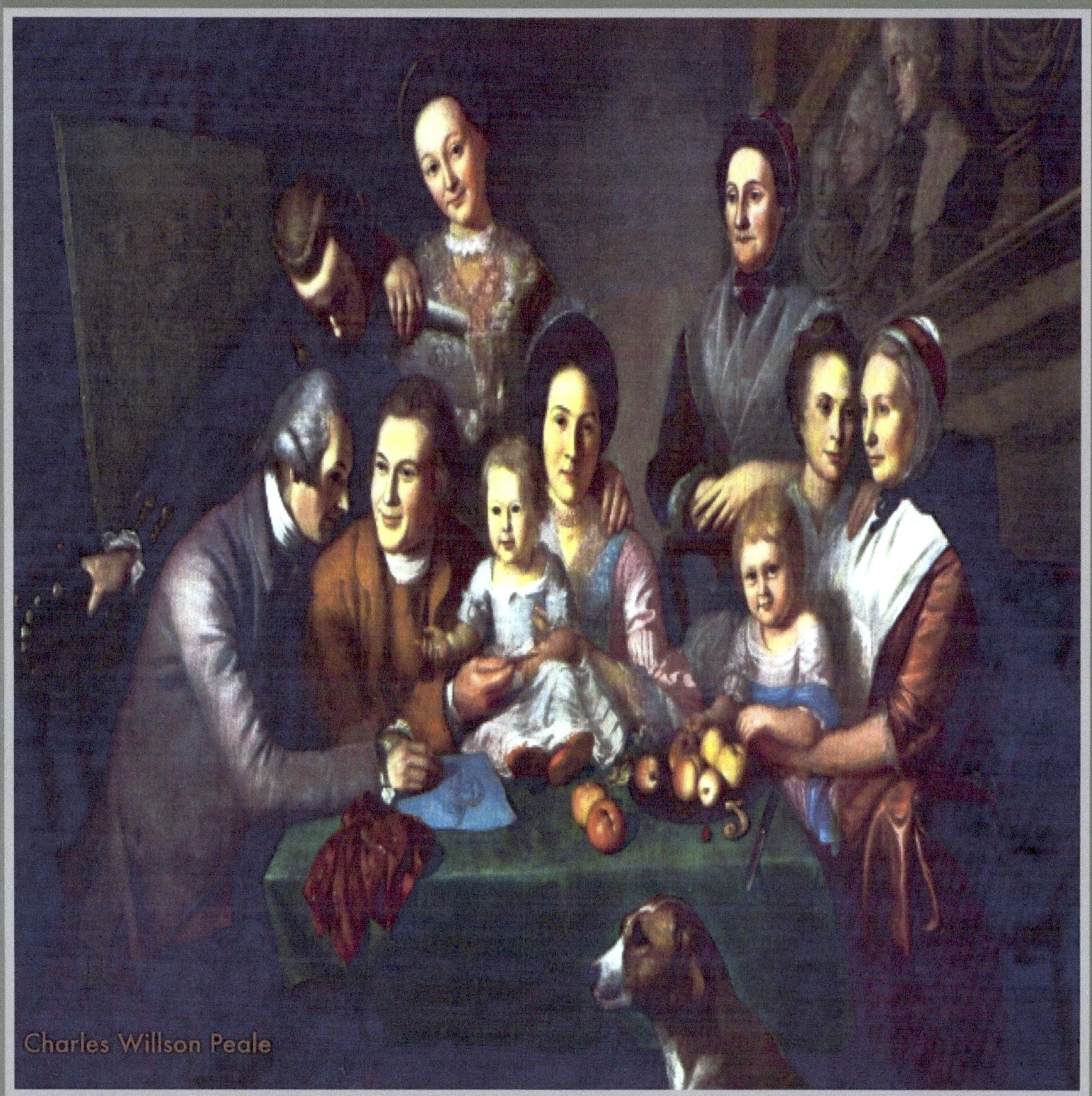
Charles Willson Peale

Without our hopes, without our fears,
Without the home that plighted love endears,
Without the smile from partial beauty won,
O! what were man? — a world without a sun.

— Campbell

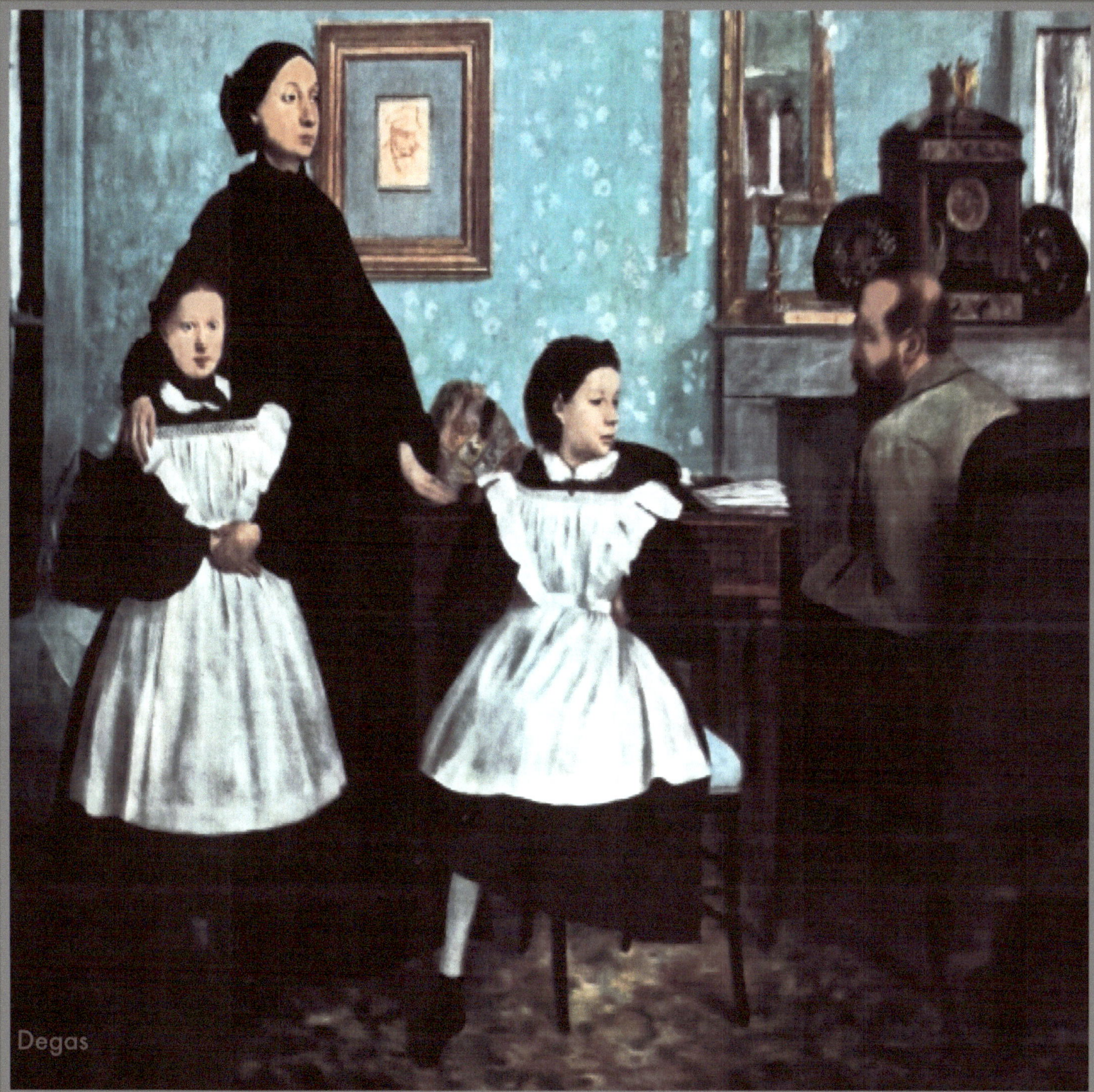
Degas

There may be beings, thinking beings,
near or surrounding us, which we do
not perceive, which we cannot imagine.
We know very little; but, in my opinion,
we know enough to hope for the immortality,
the individual immortality, of the better part of man.

– Sir H. Davy

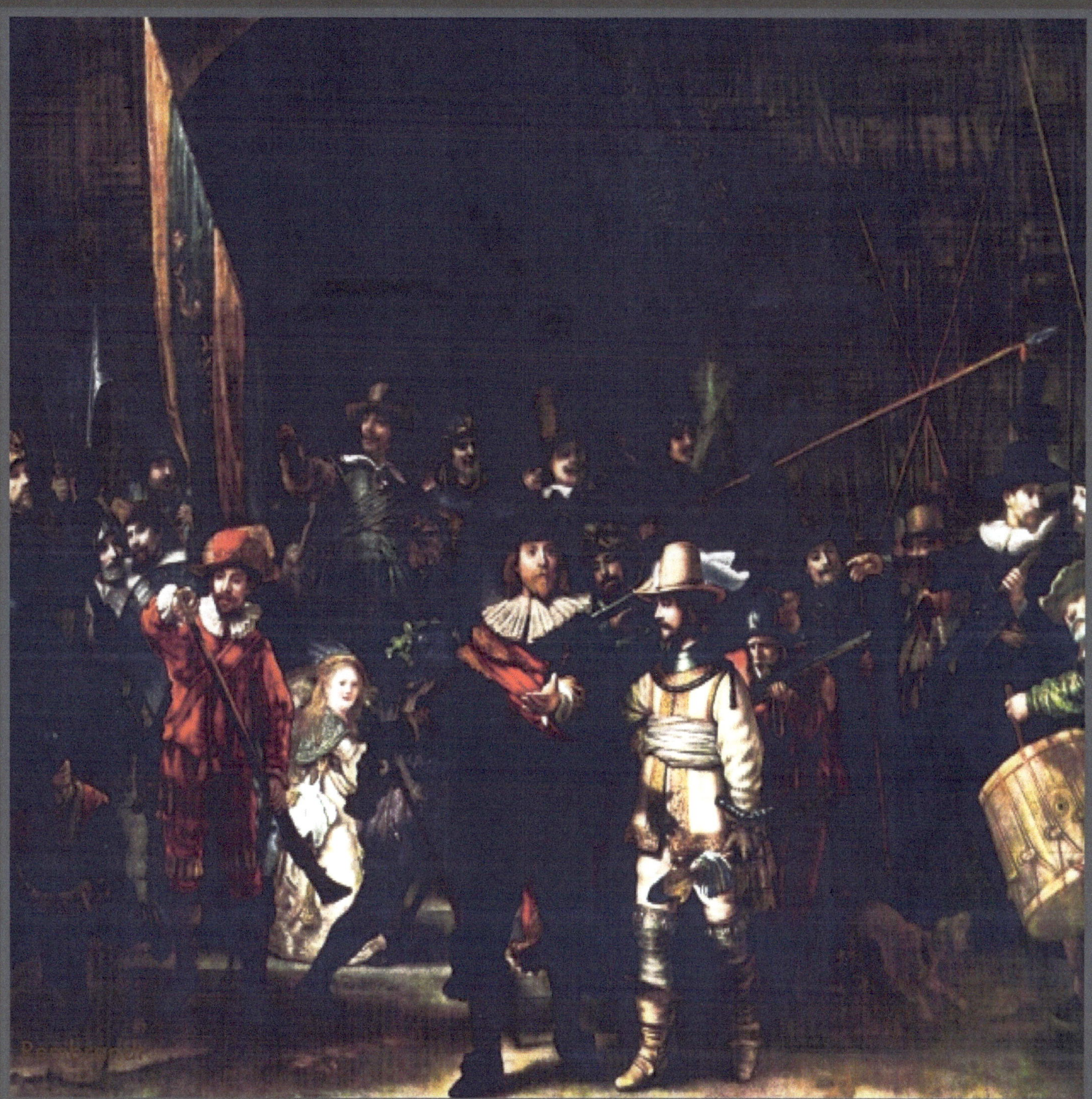

God endowed and set us for a sign to testify the worth of men and the hope there is for man. It is not our national prosperity, great as it is, that is the appropriate theme of our most joyful congratulations, but it is our success in demonstrating that men are equal as God's children, which affords a prophecy of better things for the race.

— Leonard Bacon

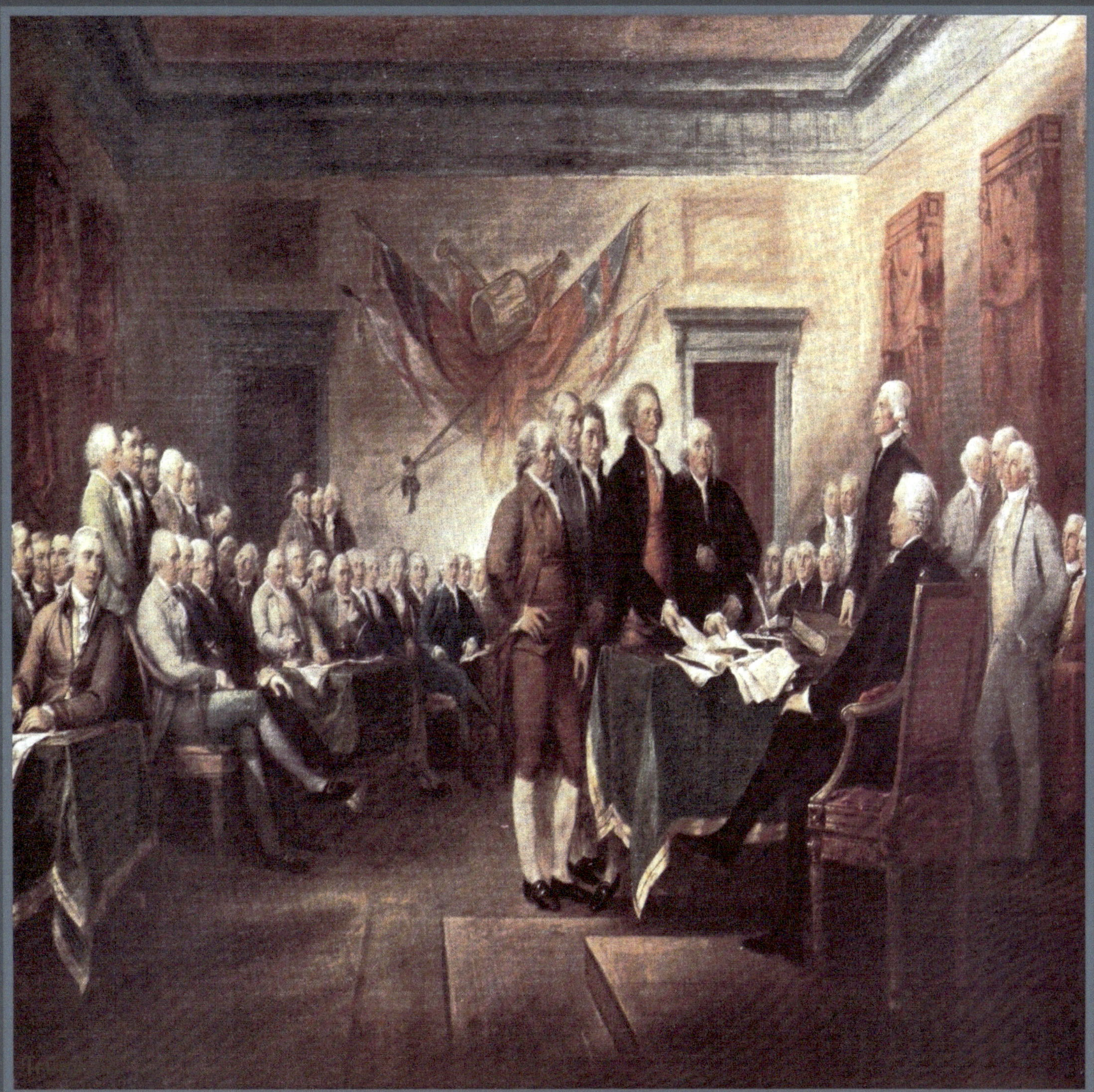

Love, hope, and joy, fair pleasure's smiling train.
Hate, fear, and grief, the family of pain;
These, mix'd with art, and to due bound! confin'd,
Make and maintain the balance of the mind:
The lights and shades, whose well-accorded strife.
Gives all the strength and color of our life.

– Pope

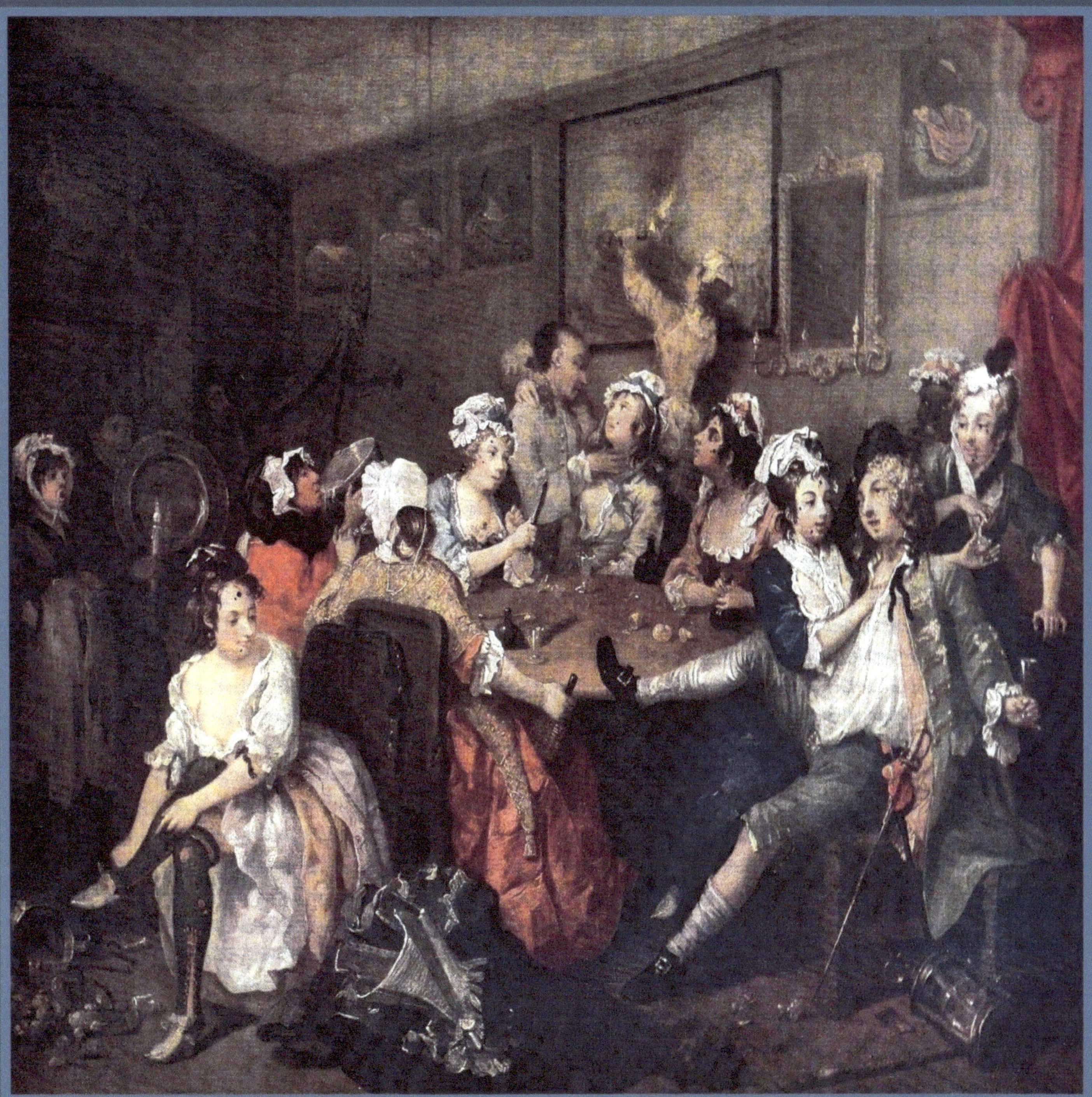

Who will not mercy unto others show,
how can he mercy ever hope to have?

—Spenser

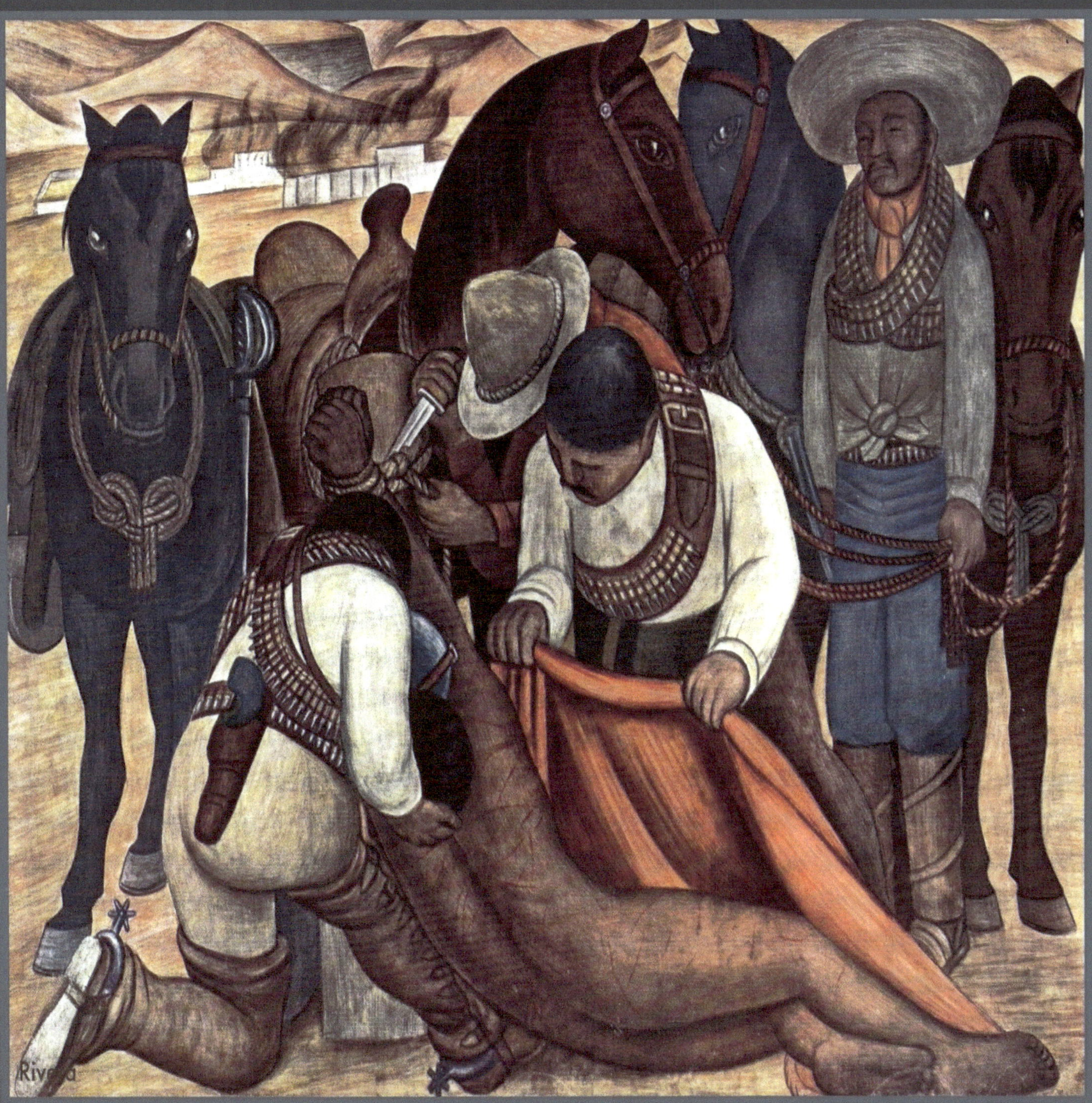

O nightingale, that on yon
blooming spray warblest at eve,
when all the woods are still,—
thou with fresh hope to lower
heart doth fill!

— Milton

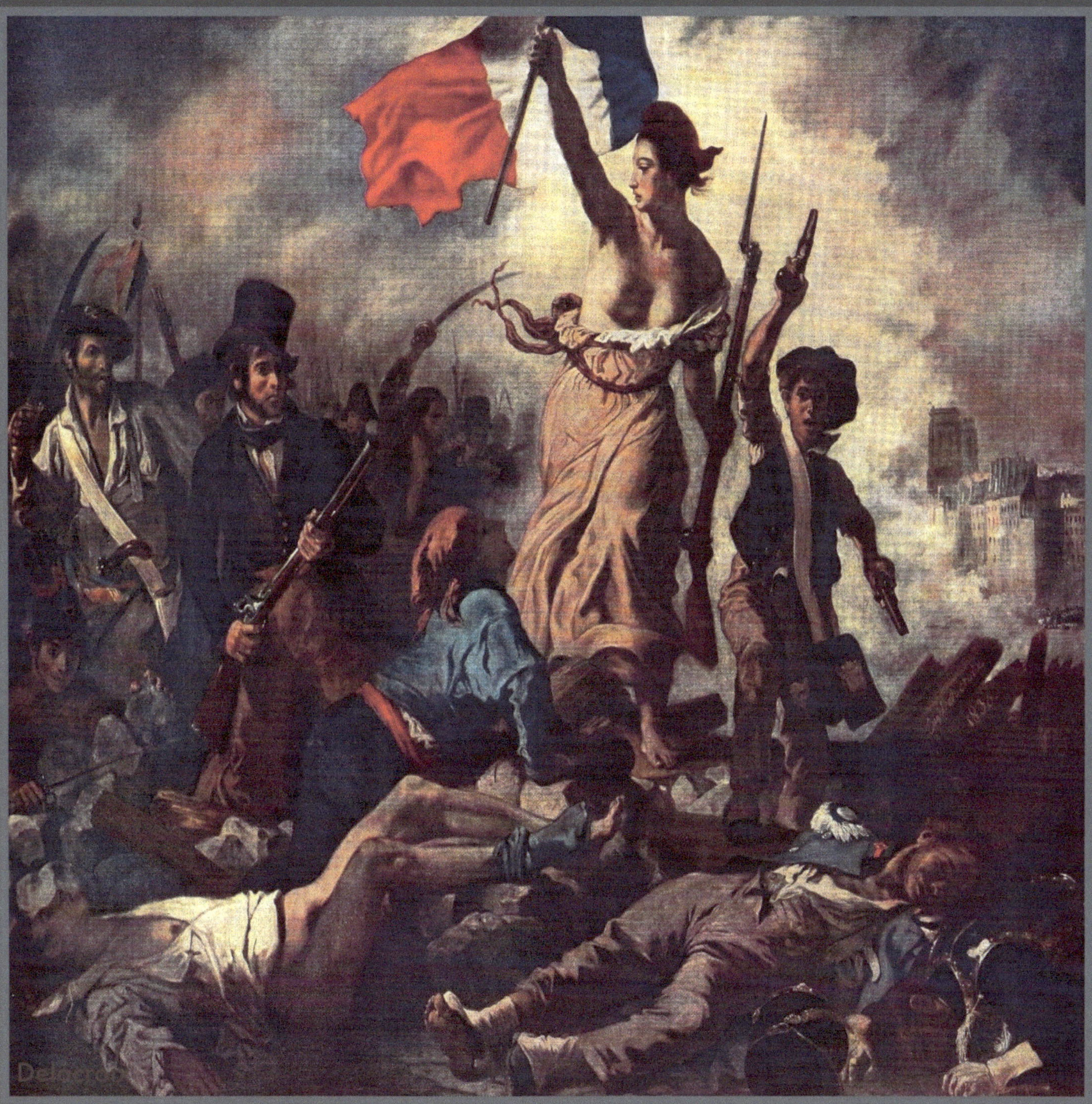

Method means primarily a way or path of transit. From this we are to understand that the first idea of method is a progressive transition from one step to another in any course. If in the right course, it will be the true method; if in the wrong, we cannot hope to progress.

– Coleridge

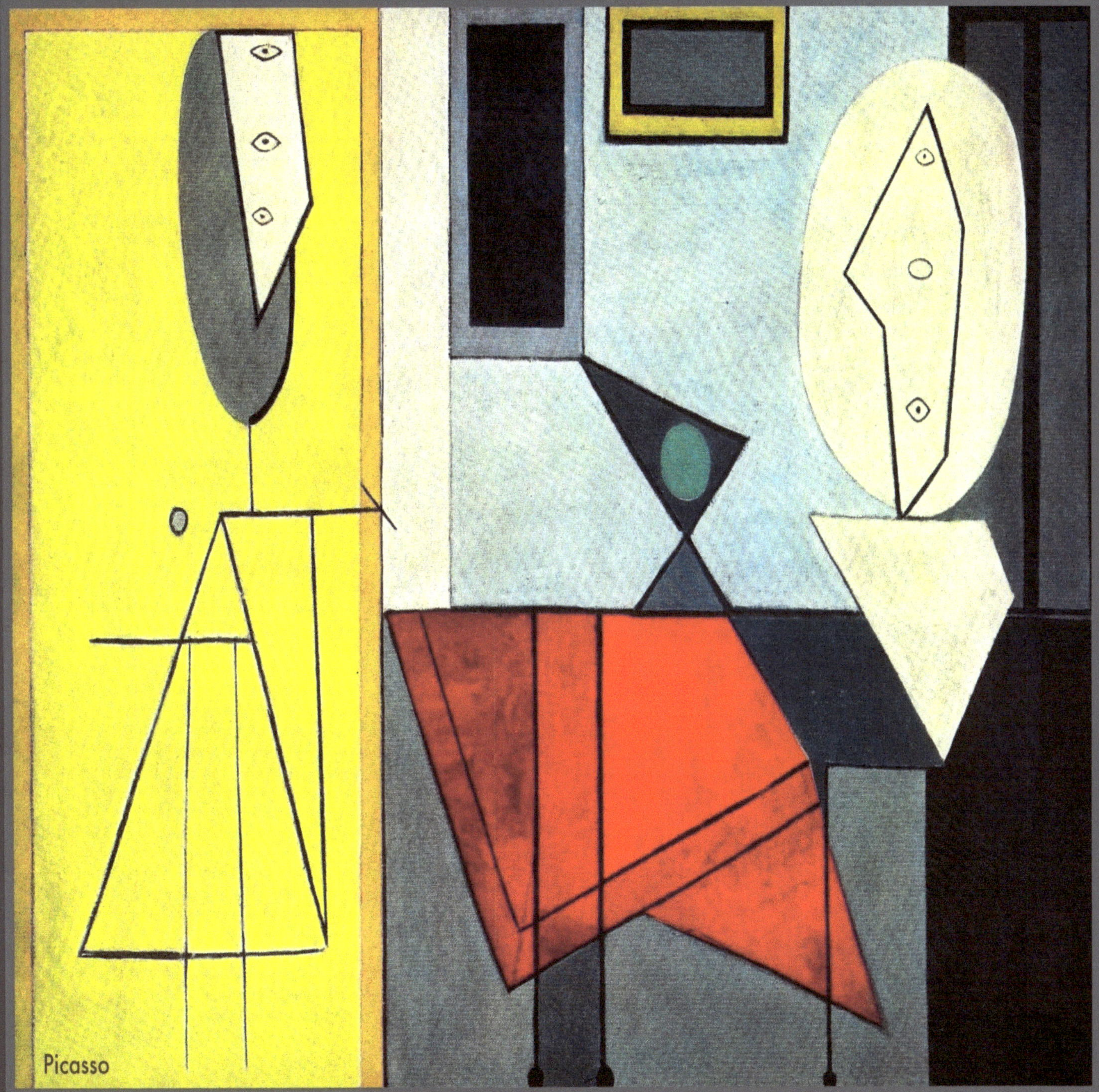
Picasso

There is no life so humble that, if it be true
and genuinely human and obedient to God,
it may not hope to shed some of His light.
There is no life so meager that the greatest
and wisest of us can afford to despise it.
We cannot know at what moment it may
flash forth with the life of God.

— Phillips Brooks

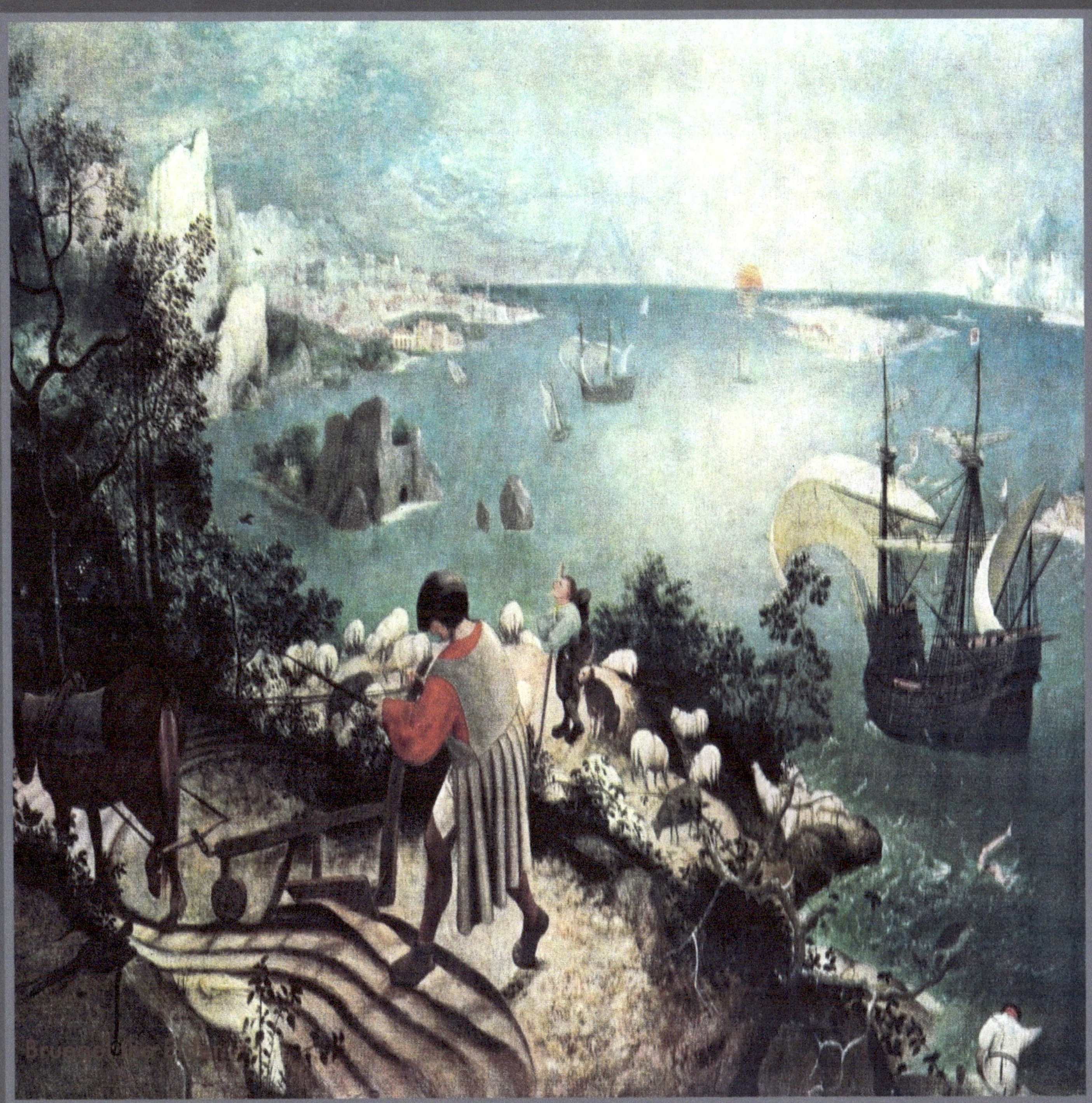

Life, unexplored, is hope's perpetual blaze -
When past, one long, involved, and dark - some maze:
But, that some mighty power controls the whole,
A secret intuition tells the soul.

— William Winter

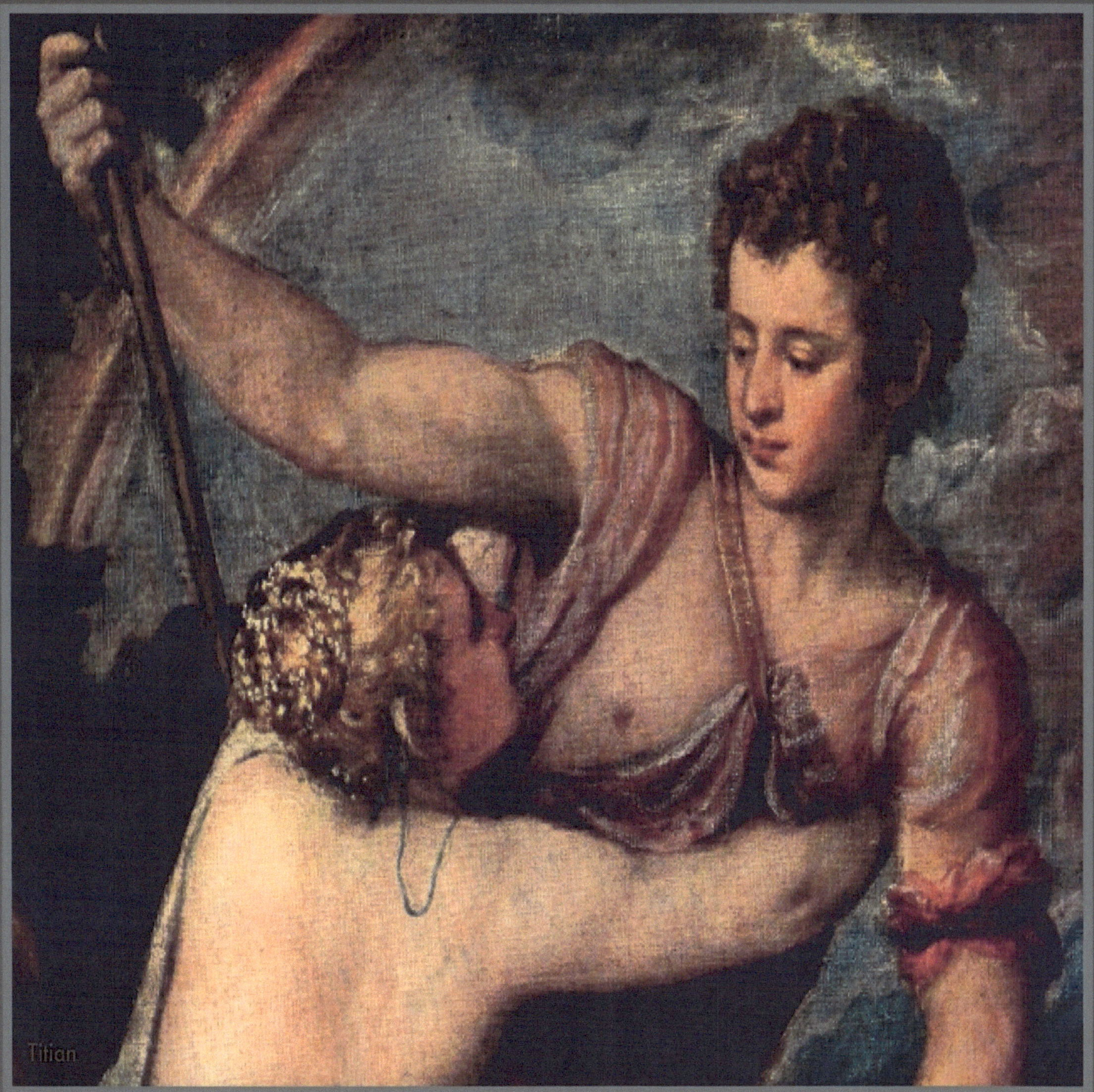
Titian

Affection can withstand very severe storms of rigor, but not a long polar frost of downright indifference. Love will subsist on wonderfully little hope, but not altogether without it.

— Walter Scott

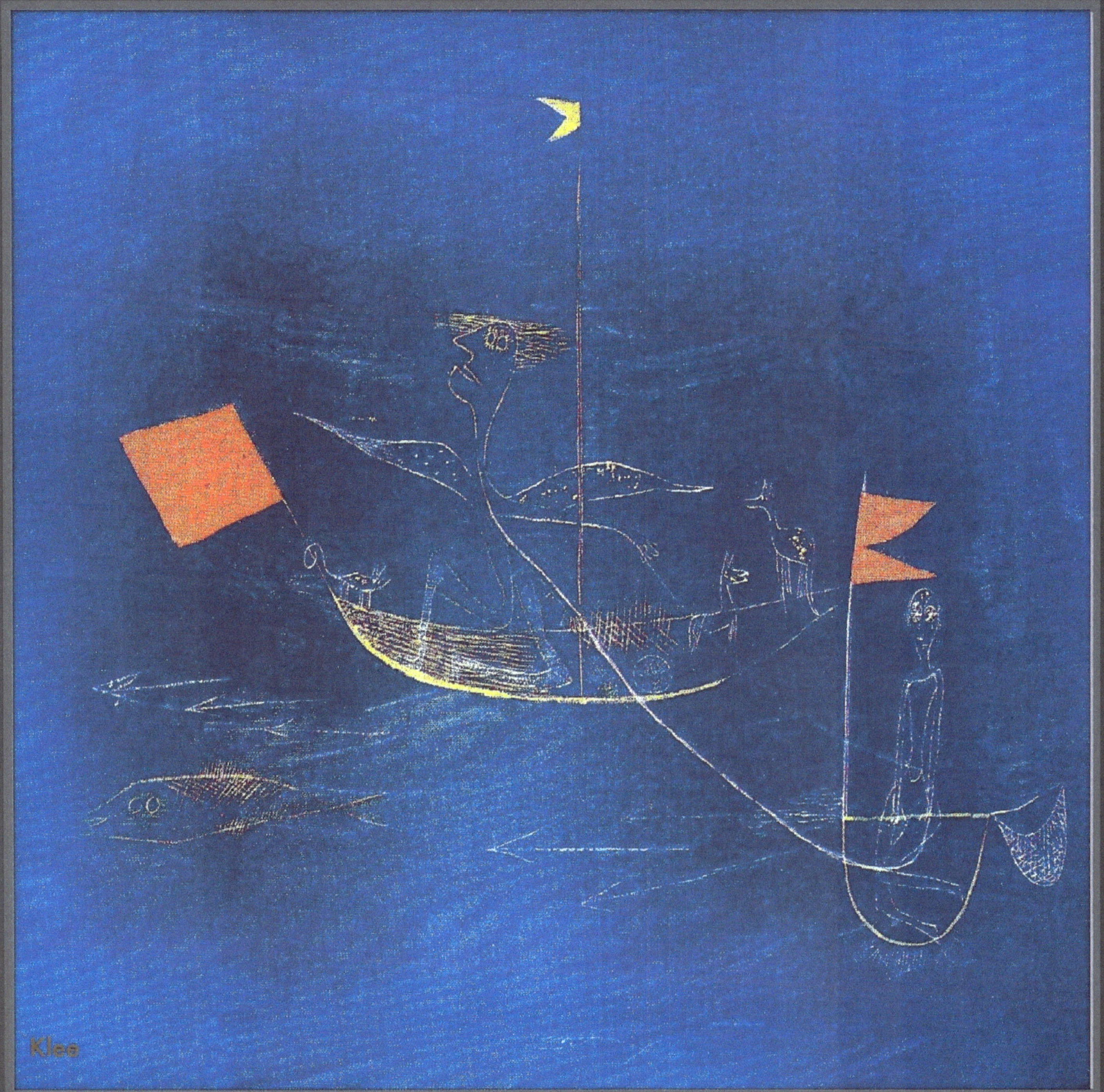
Klee

Man is an animal, formidable both from his passions and his reasons; his passions often urging him to great evils, and his reason furnishing means to achieve them.

To train this animal, and make him amenable to order, to inure him to a sense of justice and virtue, to withhold him from ill courses by fear, and encourage him in his duty by hopes; in short to fashion and model him for society, hath been the aim of civil and religious institutions; and, in all times, the endeavor of good and wise men.

The aptest method for attaining this end hath been always judged a proper education.

— Bishop Berkely

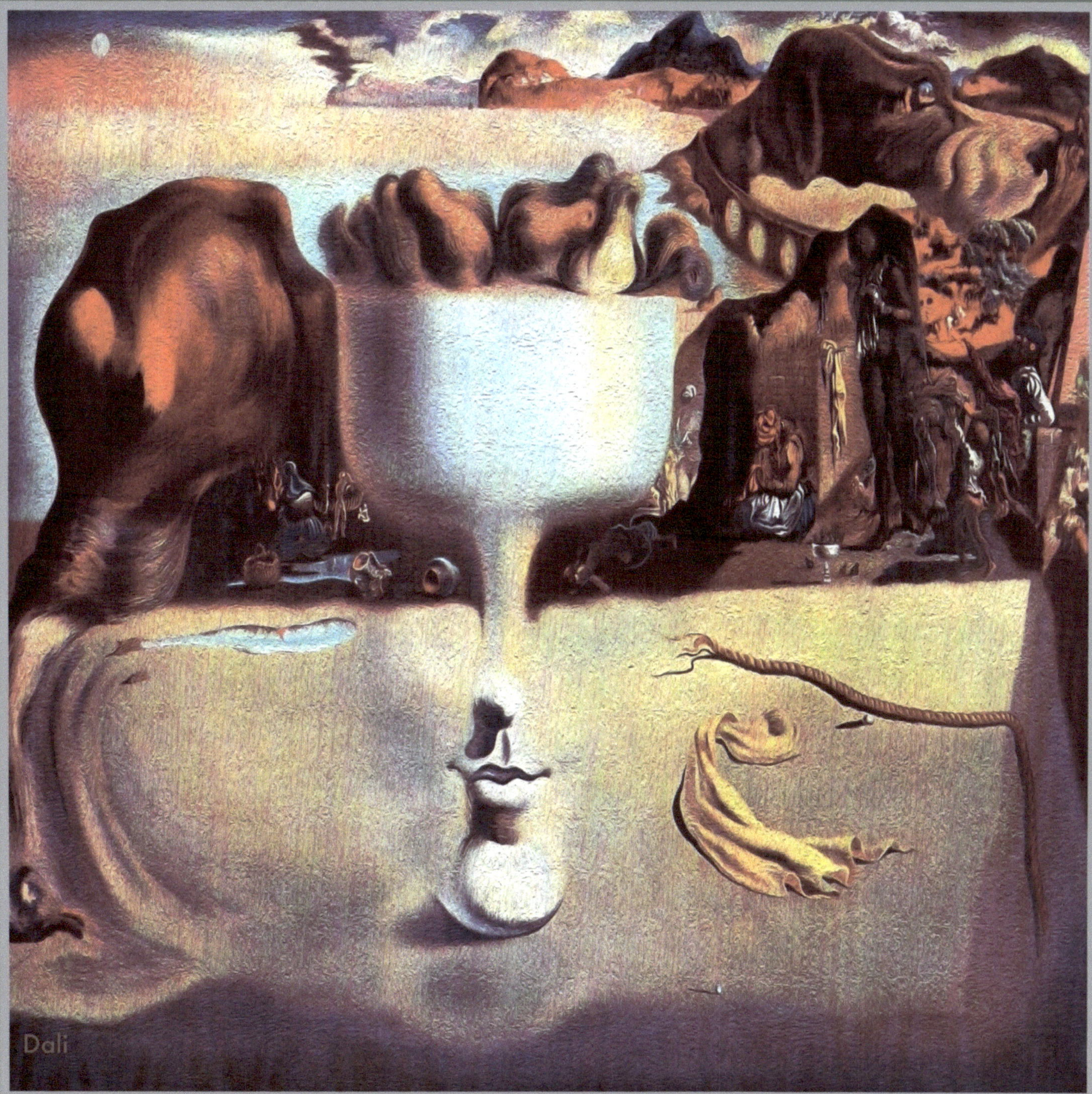

Dali

Obstinacy in opinions
holds the dogmatist in the
chains of error, without
hope of emancipation.

— Glanvill

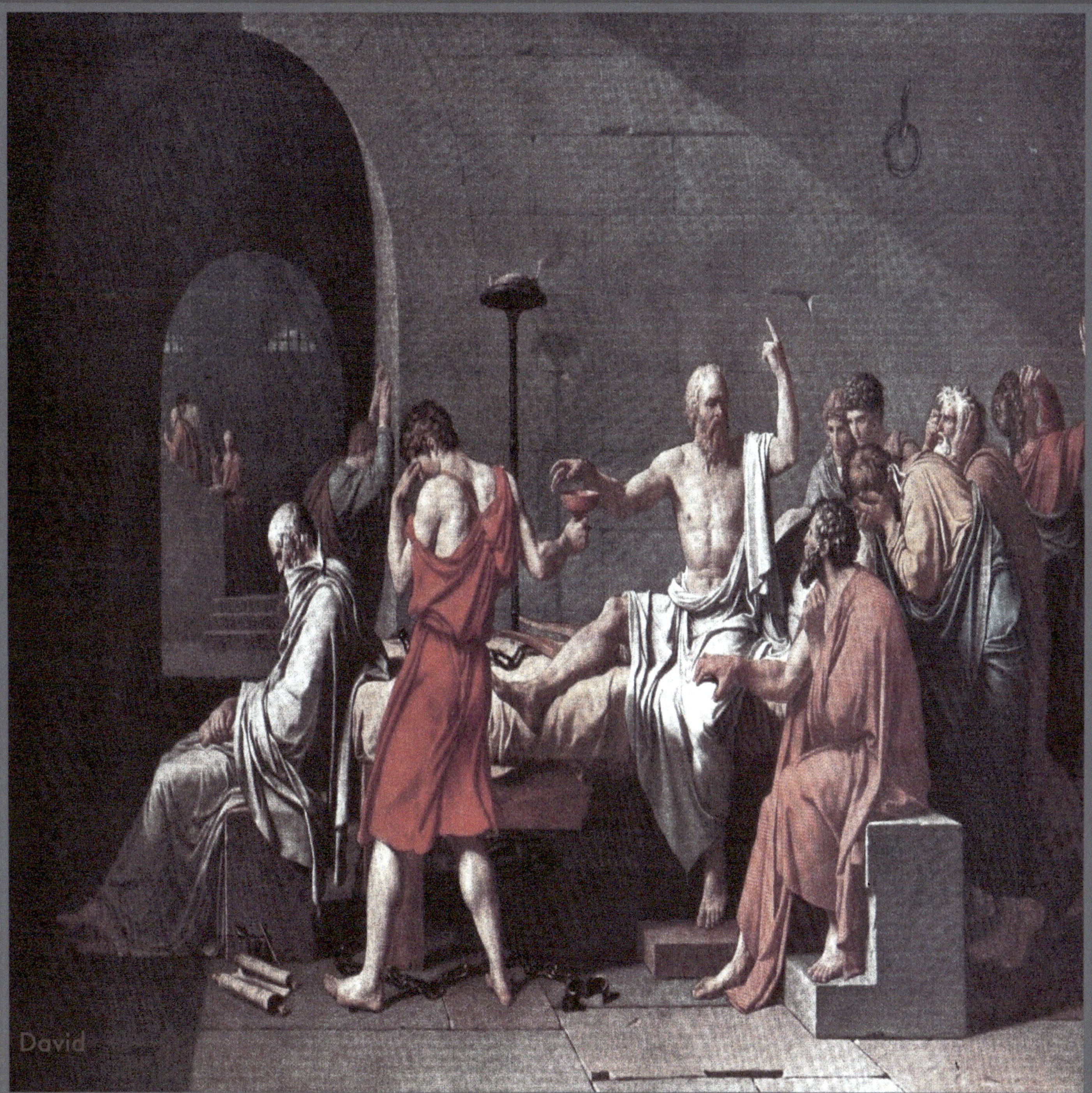
David

Interest makes some people blind and
others quick-sighted.
We promise according to our hopes,
and perform according to our fears.
Virtues are lost in interest, as rivers
are swallowed up in the sea.

— J. Beaumont

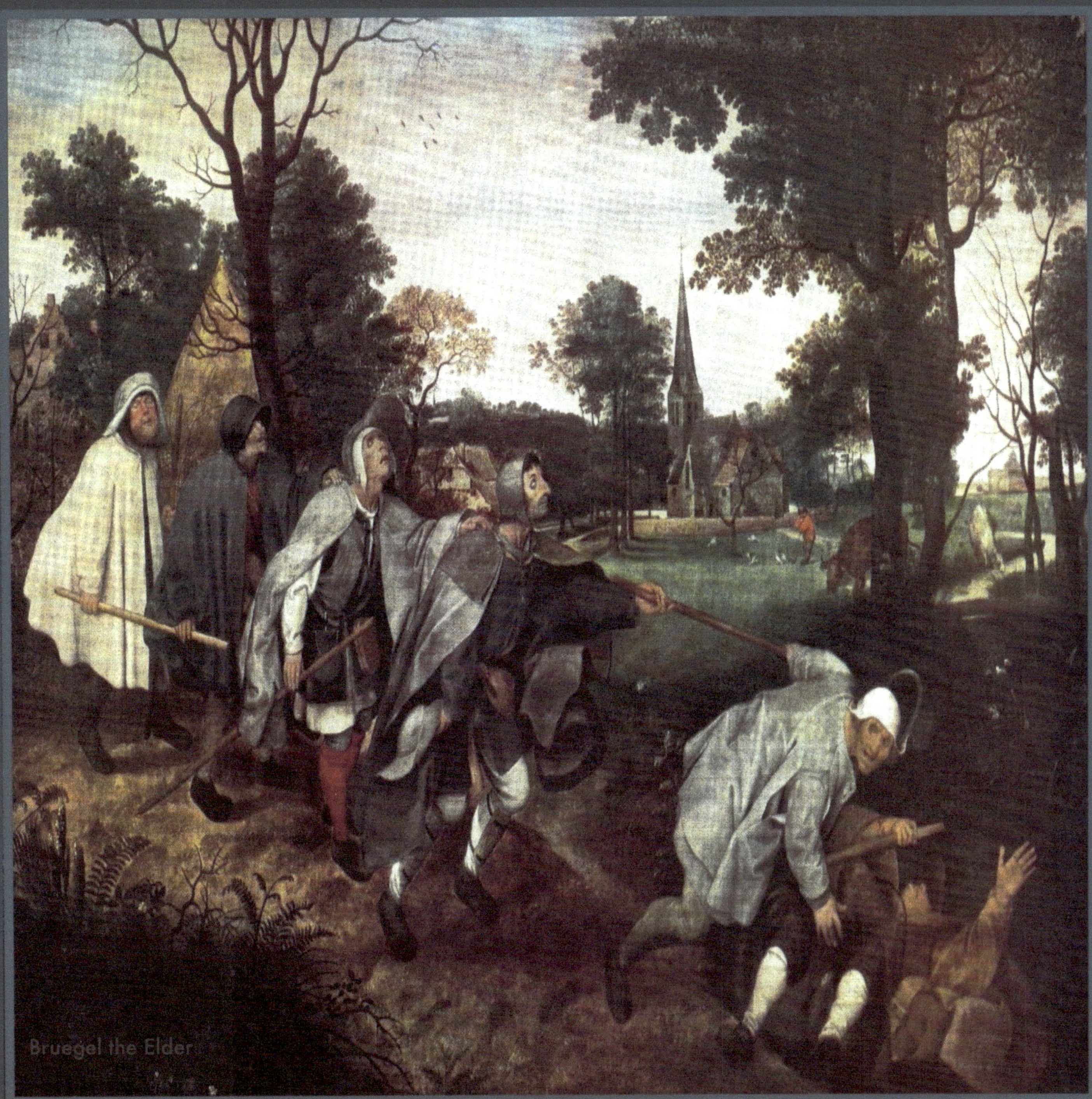

Bruegel the Elder

It is not possible to found a lasting power upon injustice, perjury, and treachery. These may, perhaps, succeed for once, and borrow for awhile, from hope, a gay and flourishing appearance. But time betrays their weakness, and they fall into ruin of themselves.
For, as instructures of every kind, the lower parts should have the greatest firmness — so the grounds and principles of actions should be just and true.

— Demosthenes

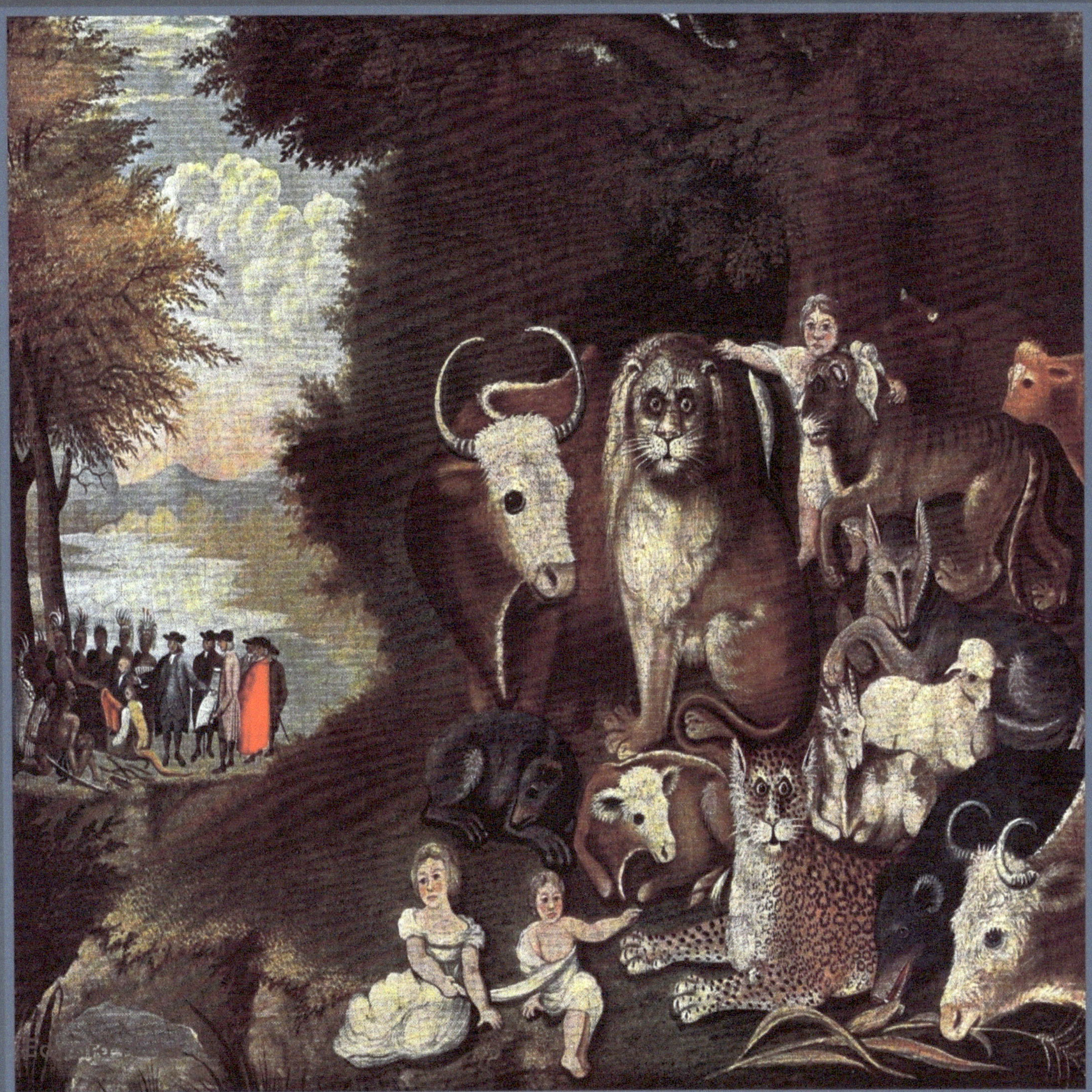

Things unhoped for happen
oftener than things we desire.

— Plautus

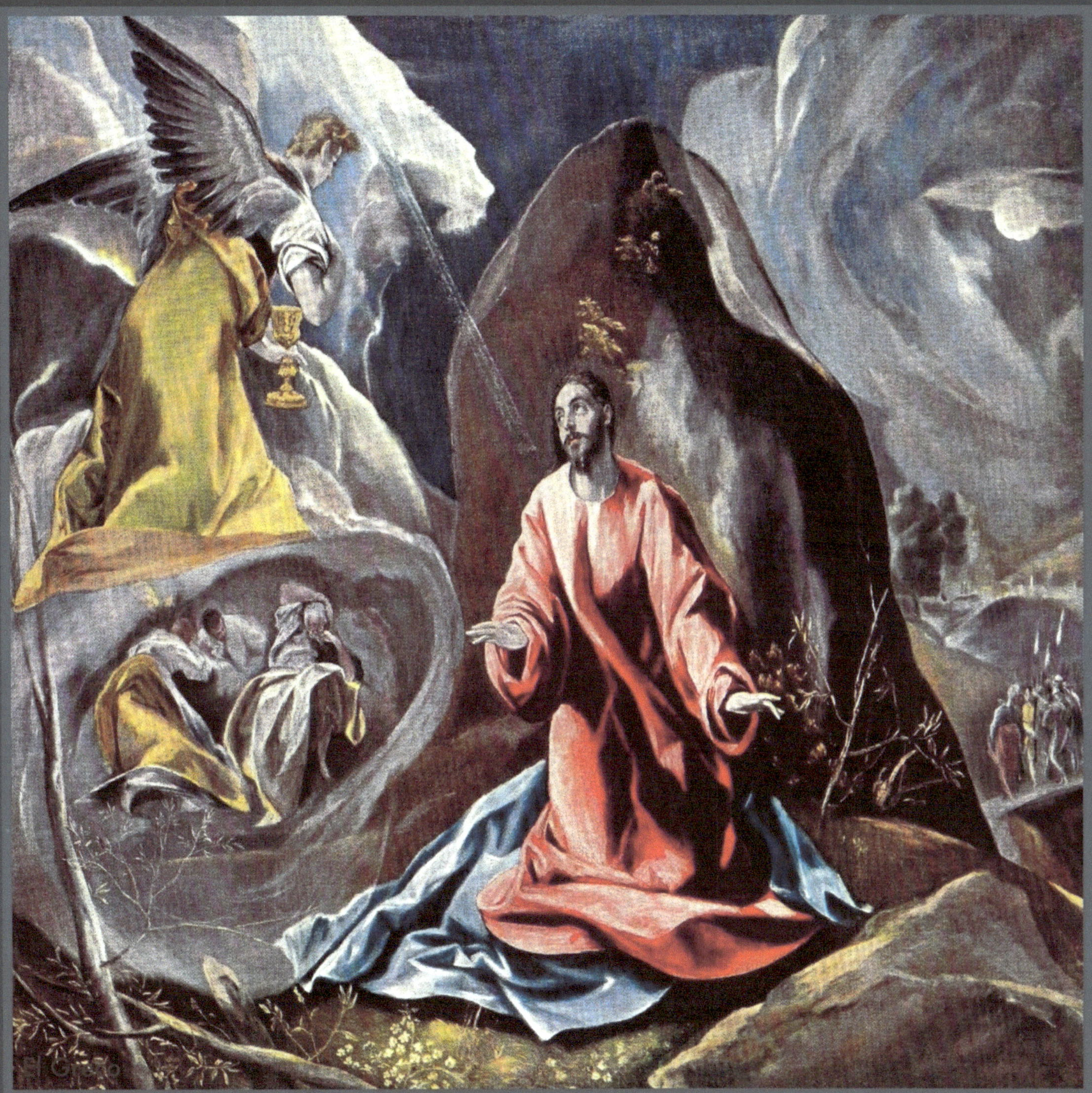

Youth fades; love droops;
the leaves of friendship fall:
A mother's secret hope
outlives them all.

— Oliver Wendell Holmes

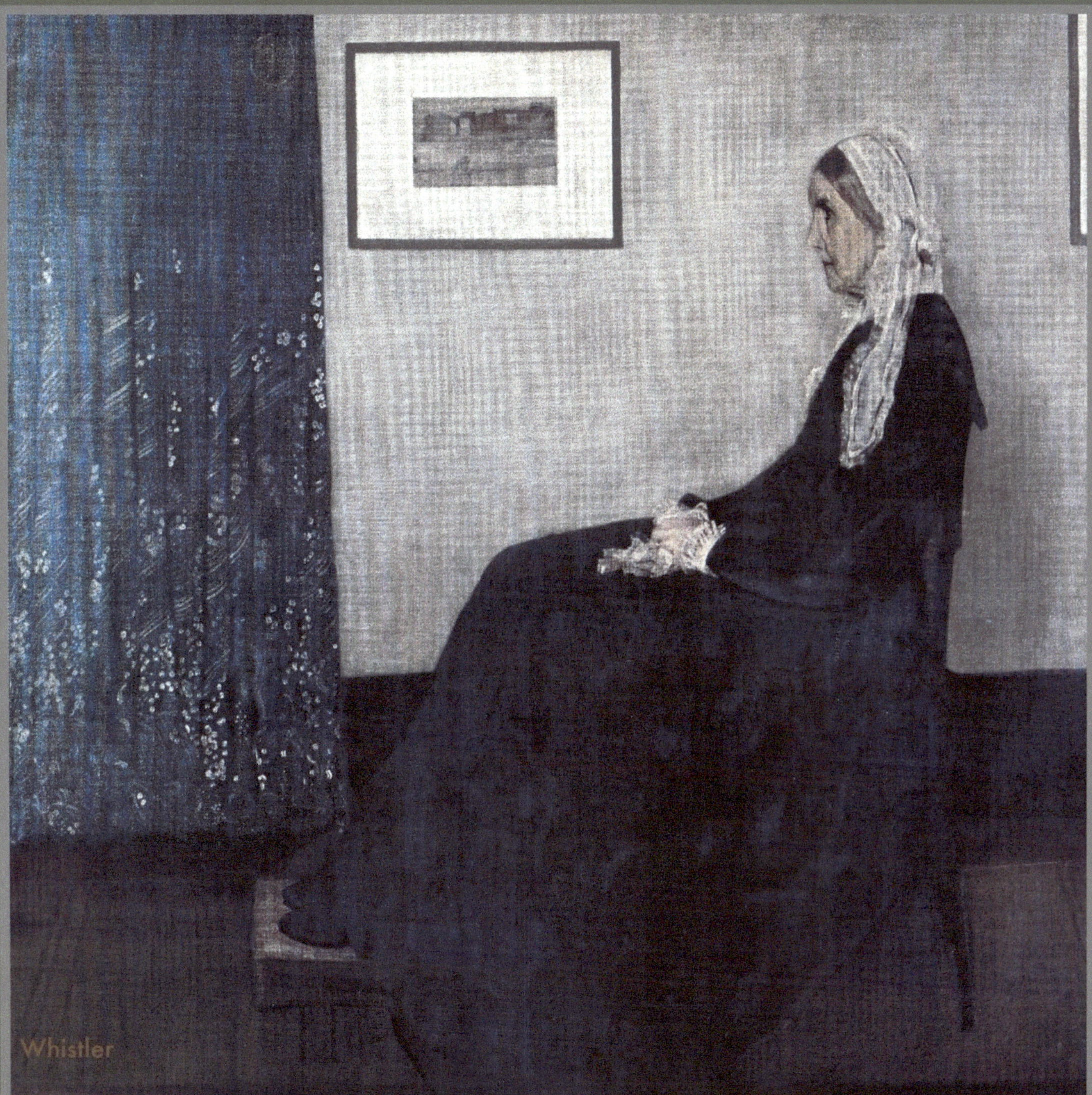
Whistler

Let the motive be in the
deed, and not in the event.
Be not one whose motive
for action is the hope of
reward.

— Krishna

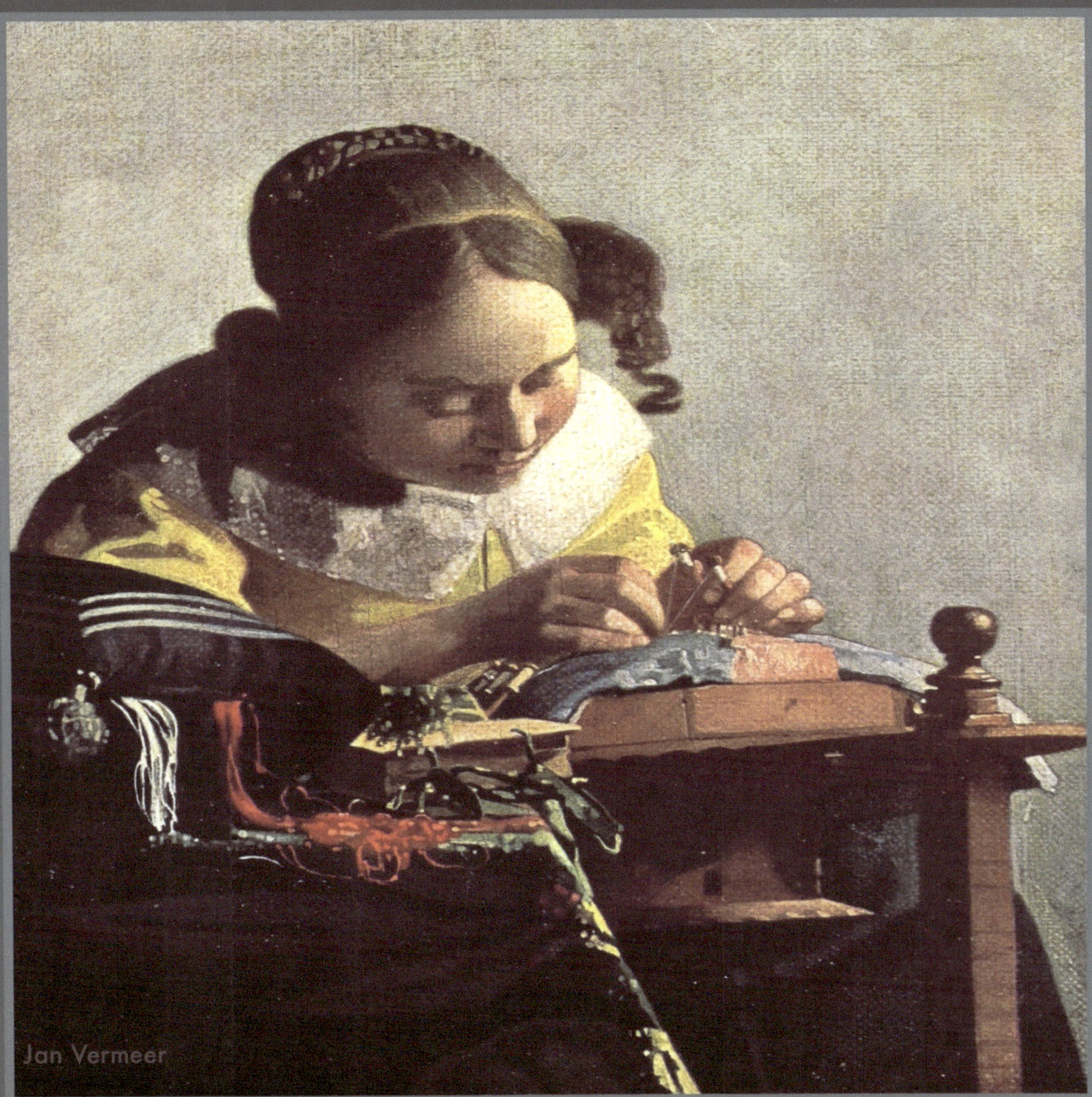
Jan Vermeer

Memory is not so brilliant
as hope, but it is more
beautiful, and a thousand
times more true.

—George D. Prentice

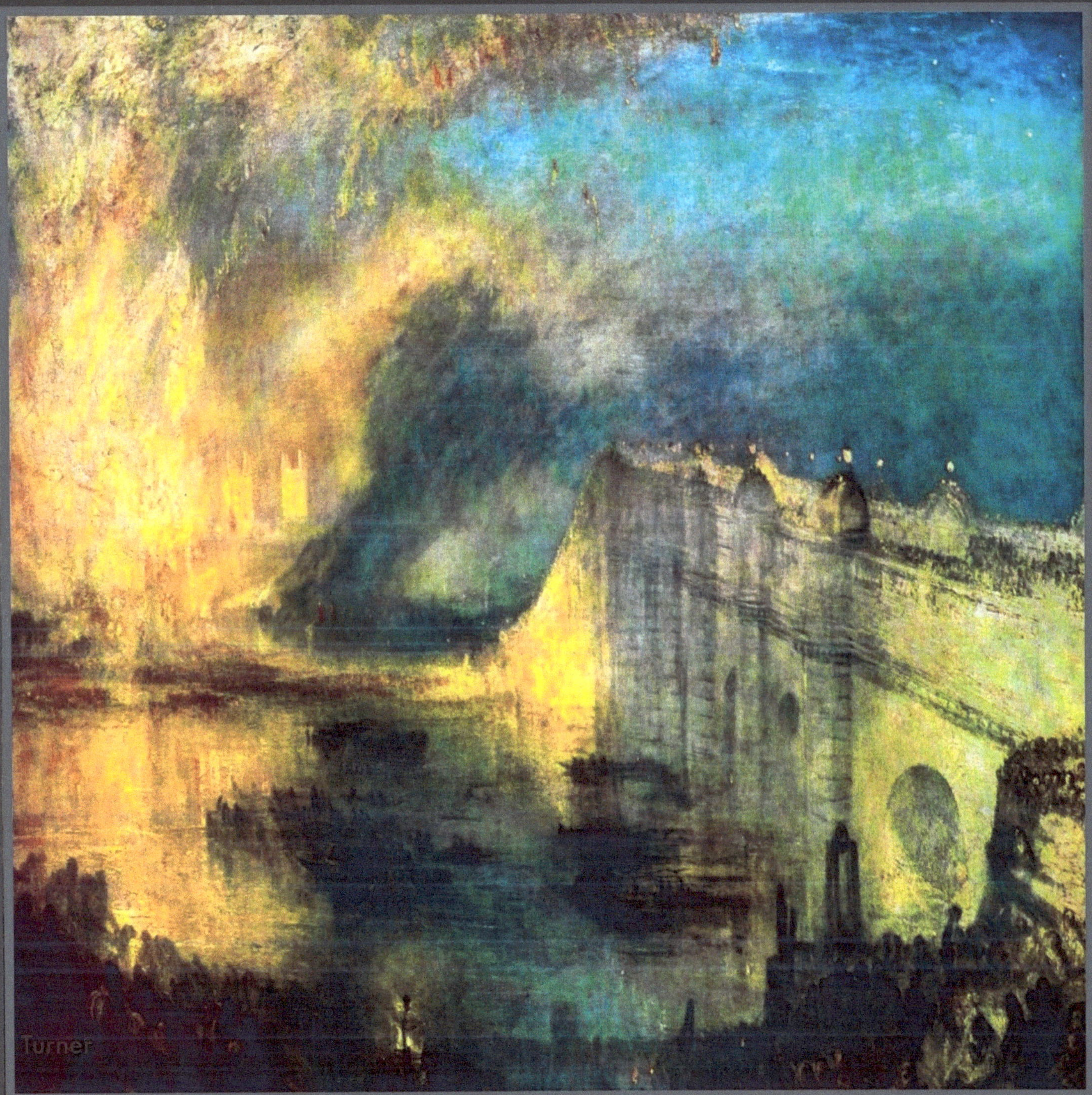
Turner

But if, indeed, there be a nobler life in us than in these strangely moving atoms; if, indeed, there is an eternal difference between the fire which inhabits them, and that which animates us,—it must be shown, by each of us in his appointed place, not merely in the patience, but in the activity of our hope, not merely by our desire, but our labor, for the time when the dust of the generations of men shall be confirmed for foundations of the gates of the city of God.

— John Ruskin

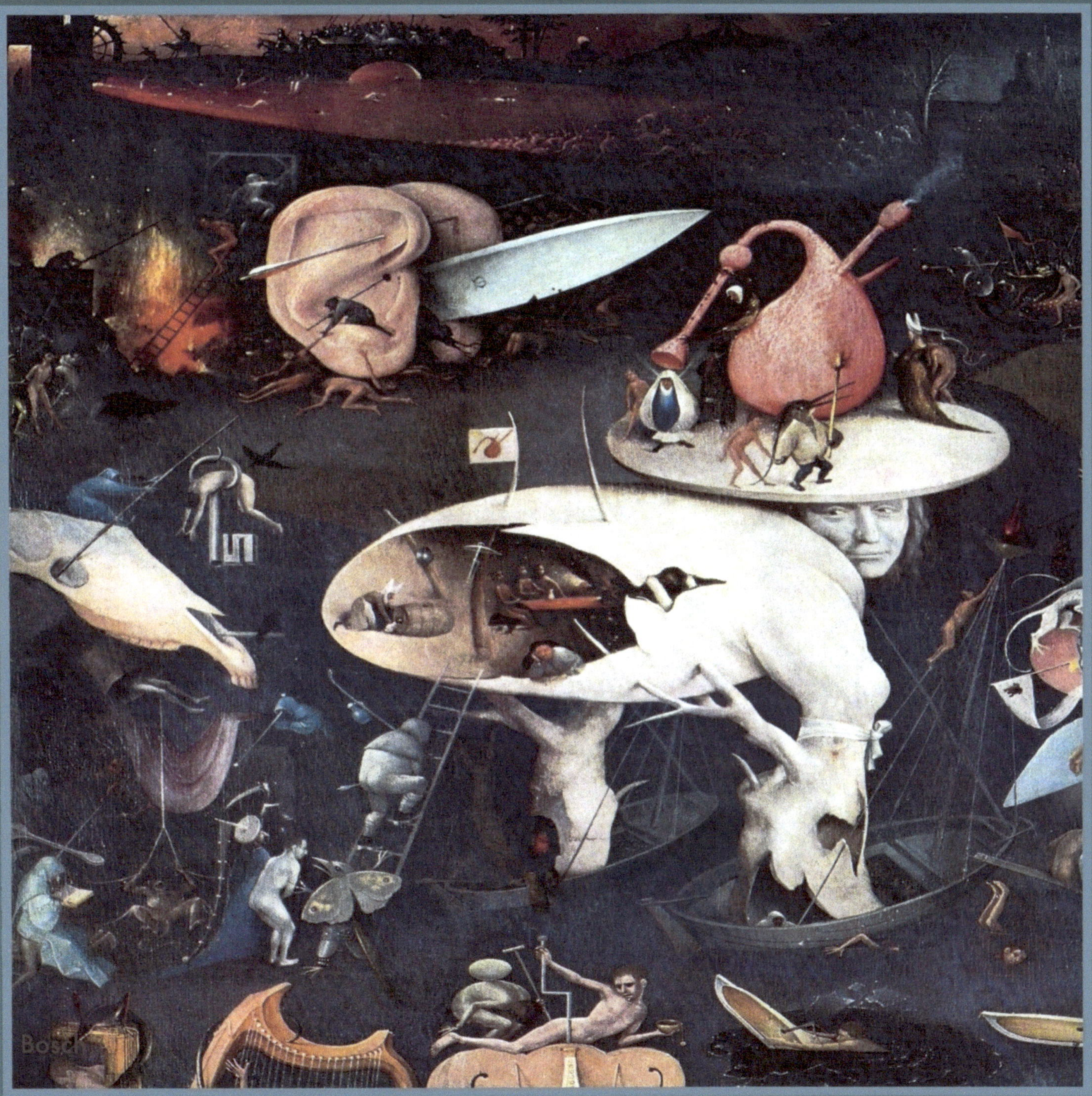
Bosch

I have great hope of a wicked man, slender hope of a mean one. A wicked man may be converted and become a prominent saint. A mean man ought to be converted six or seven times, one right after the other, to give him a fair start and put him on an equality with a bold, wicked man.

— Beecher

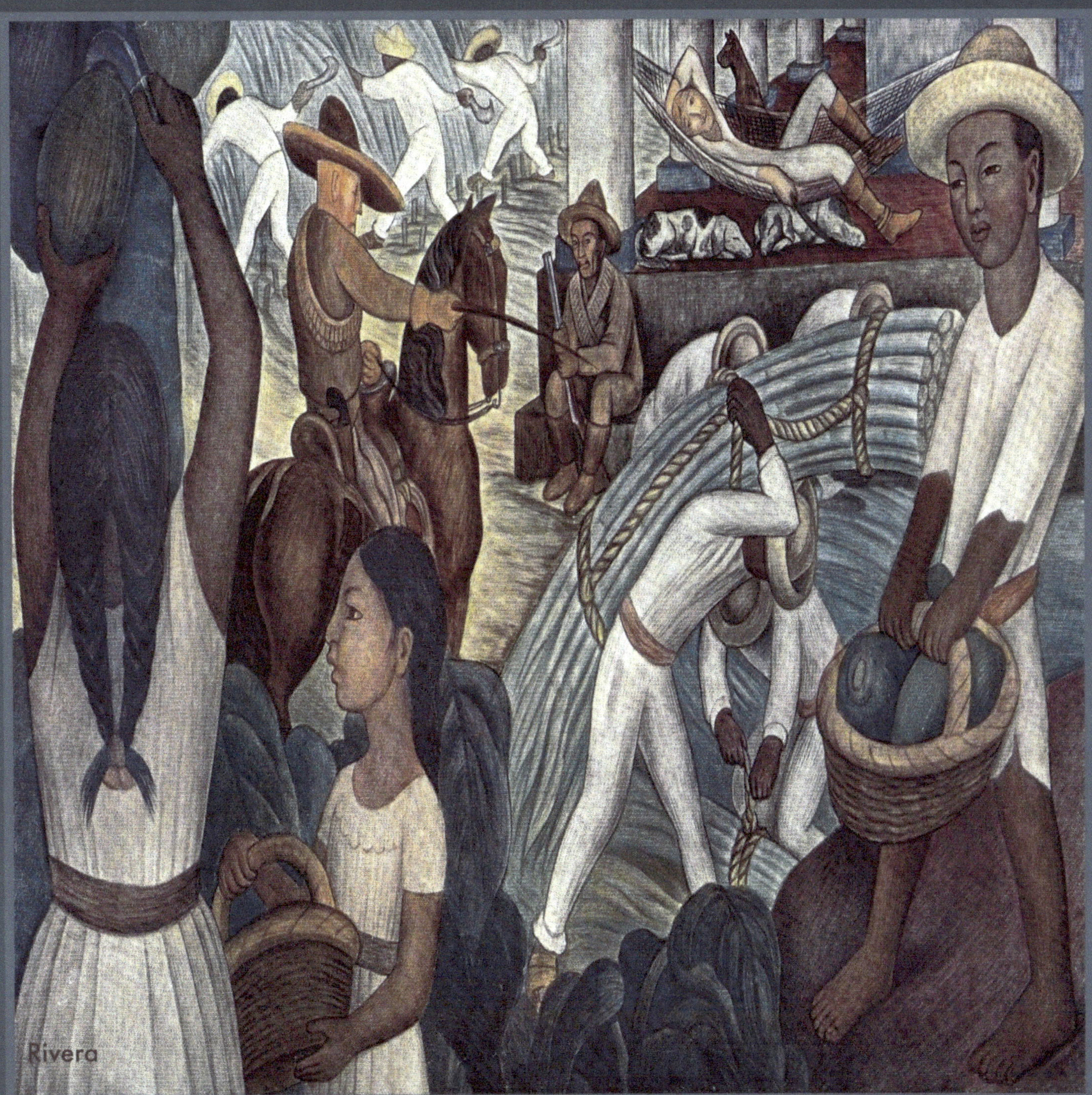
Rivera

No mother who stands upon
low ground herself can hope to
place her children upon a
loftier plane. They may reach
it, but it will not be through her.

— Julia C. R. Dorr

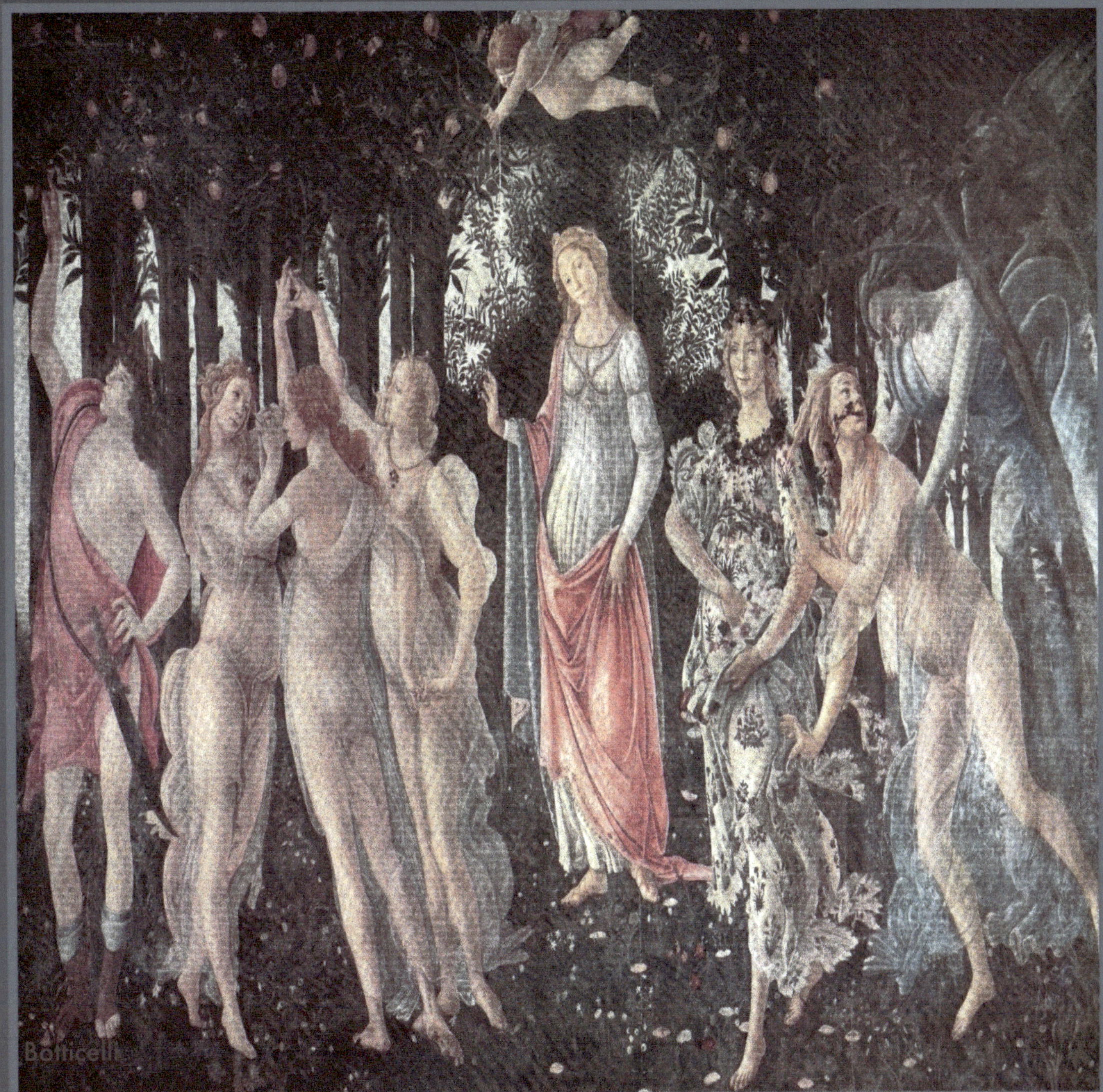
Botticelli

Marriage to maids is like
a war to men; The battle
causes fear, but the sweet
hopes of winning at the last,
still draws 'em in.

—Nat. Lee

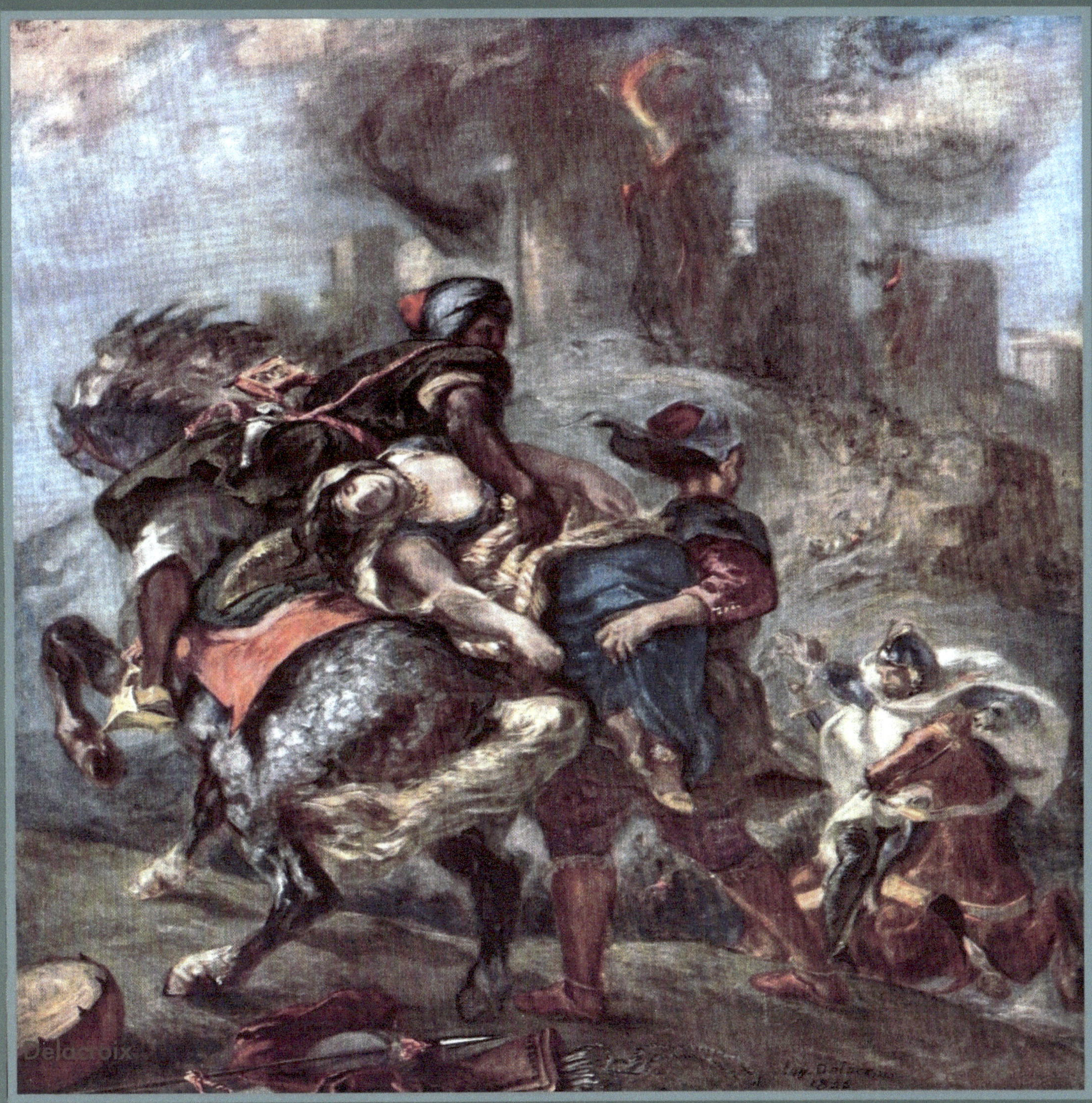
Delacroix

The young girl who begins to experience the necessity of loving seeks to hide it; but the desire of pleasing betrays the secret of her heart, and sometimes reveals her hopes.

— Beauchene

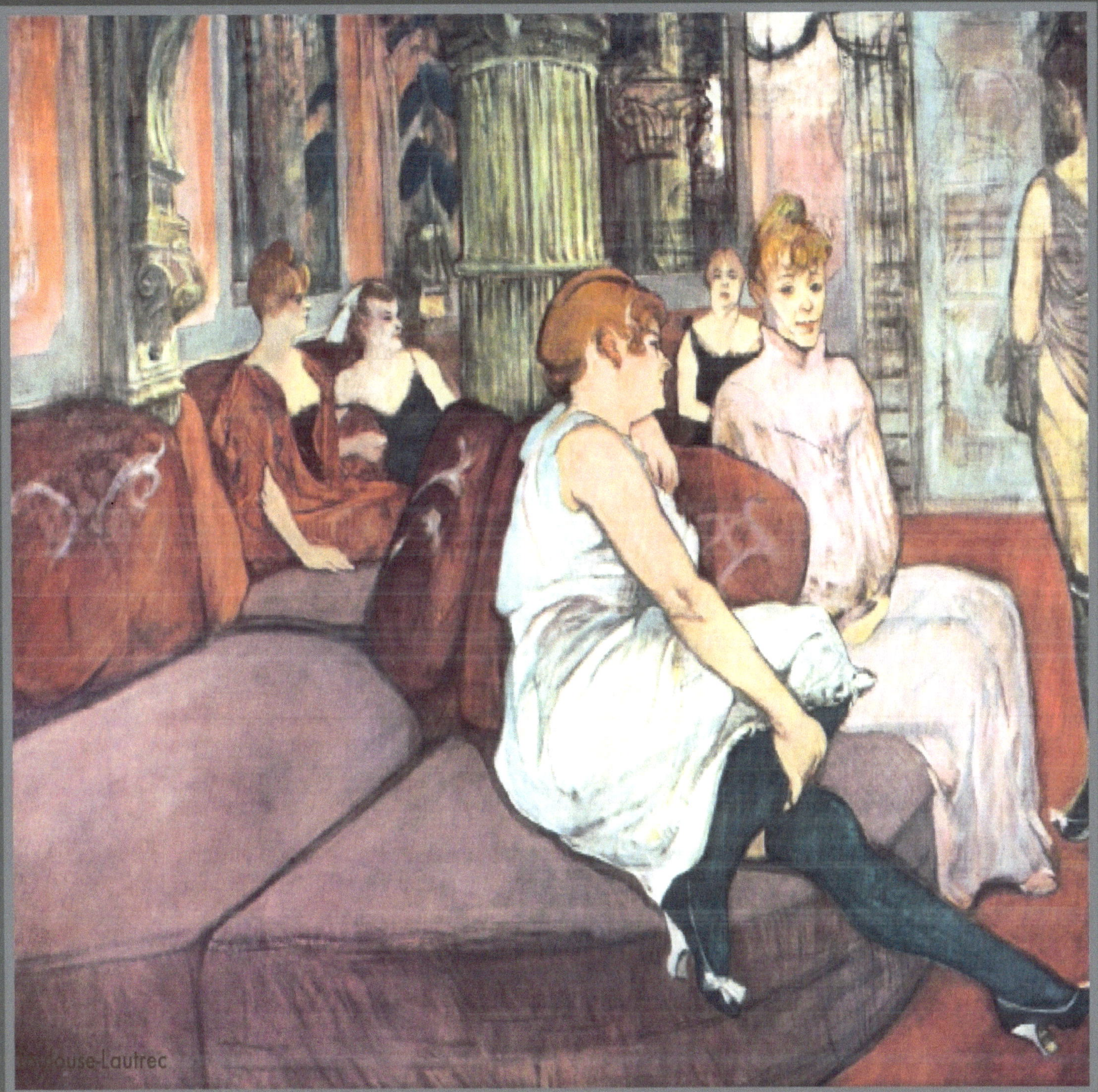
ouse-Lautrec

My own lov'd light,

That very soft and solemn spirit worships.

That lovers love so well—strange joy is thine,

Whose influence o'er all tides of soul hath power,

Who lend'st thy light to rapture and despair;

The glow of hope and wan hue of sick fancy

Alike reflect thy rays: alike thou lightest

The path of meeting or of parting love—

Alike on mingling or on breaking hearts

Thou smil'st in throned beauty!

— Maturin

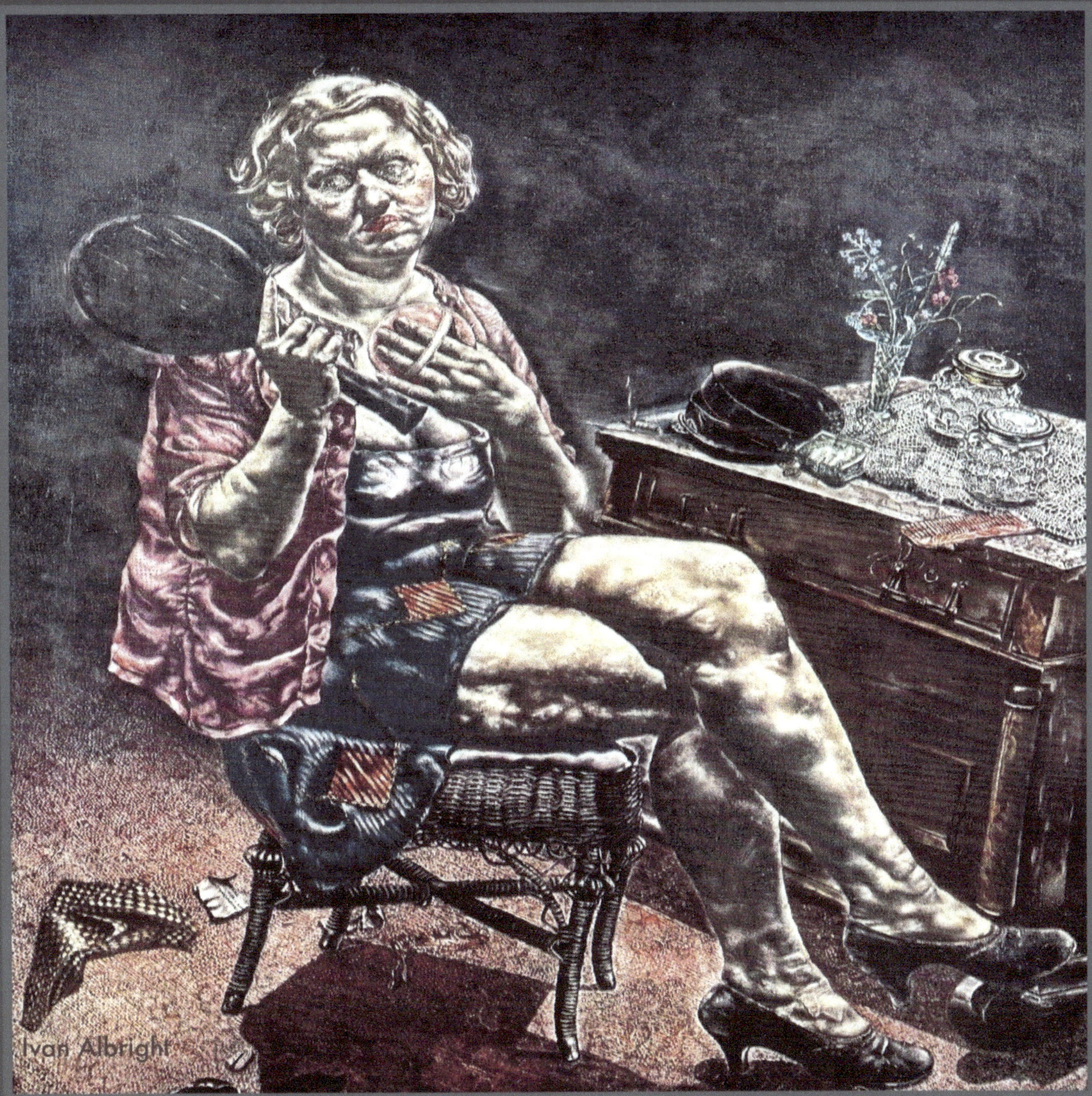
Ivan Albright

Men of dissolute lives have little incentive to look forward to the hopes and glories of immortality. A due conception of these would be incompatible with such a life.

— Beecher

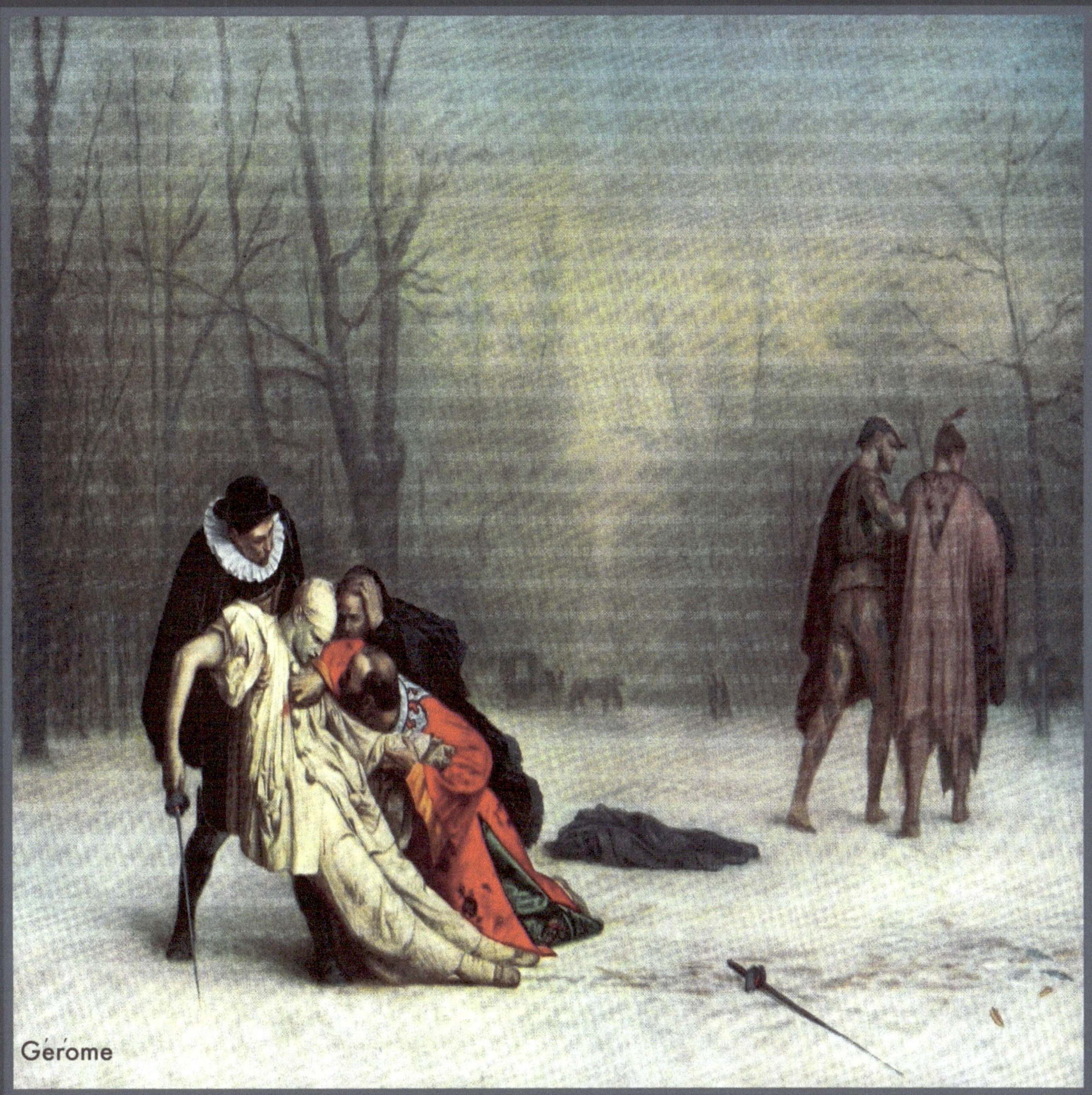

Gérome

The history of mankind is
little else than a narrative of
designs which have failed,
and hopes that have been
disappointed.

—Johnson

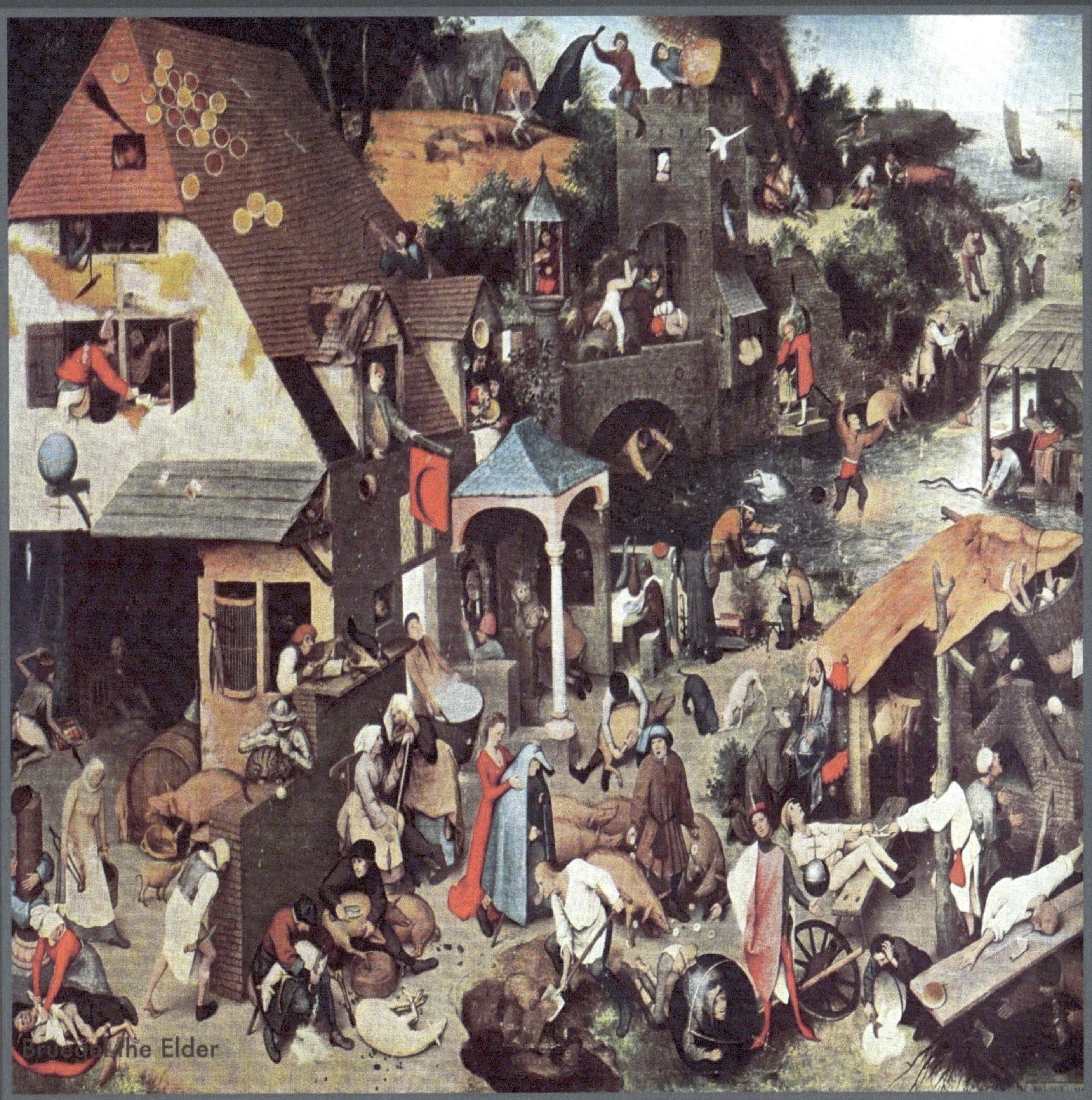
he Elder

Never let your hopes stop short of the eternal home.

— Cottager and Artisan

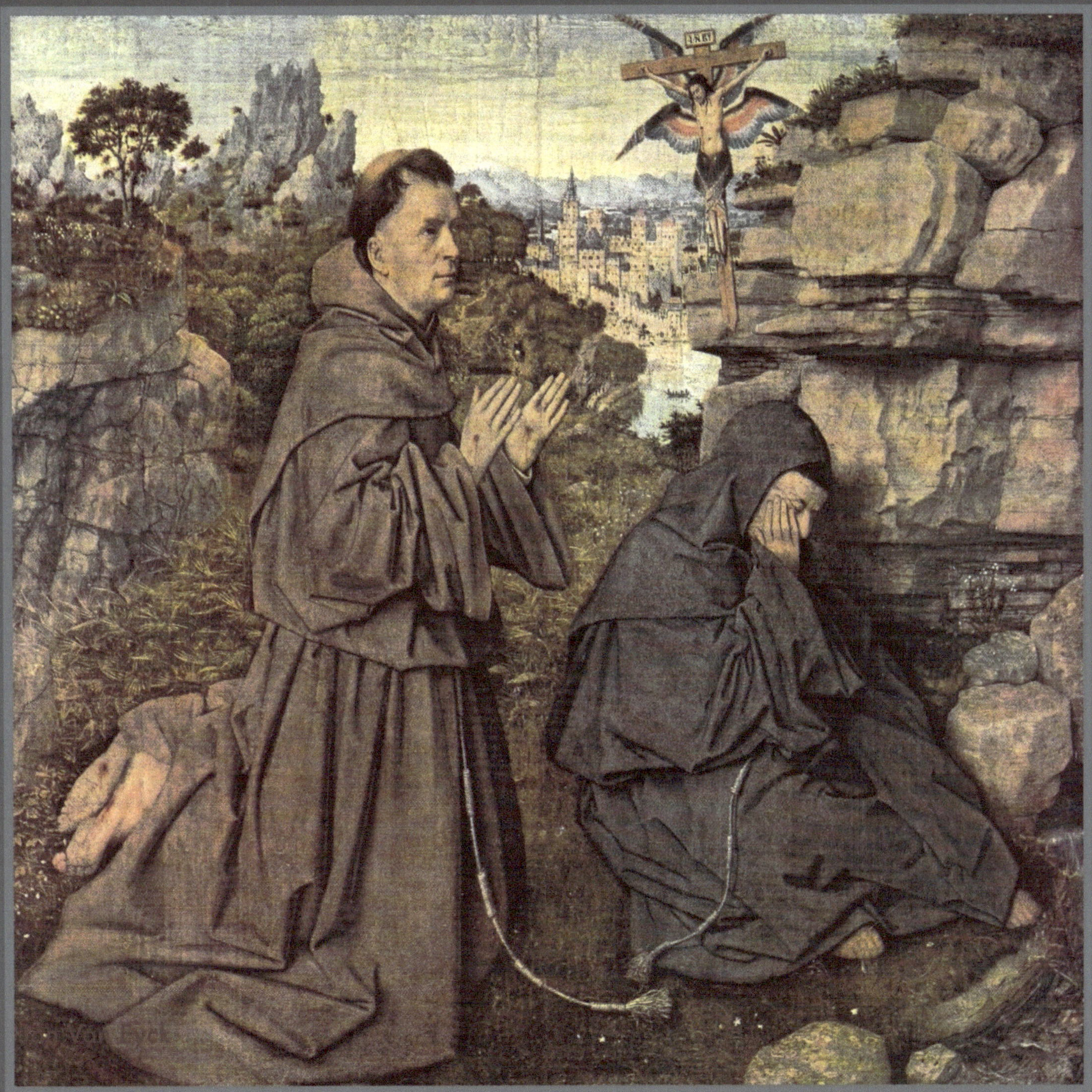

Hope nothing from luck; and the probability is that you will be so prepared, forewarned, and forearmed that all shallow observers will call you lucky.

— Bulwer-Lytton

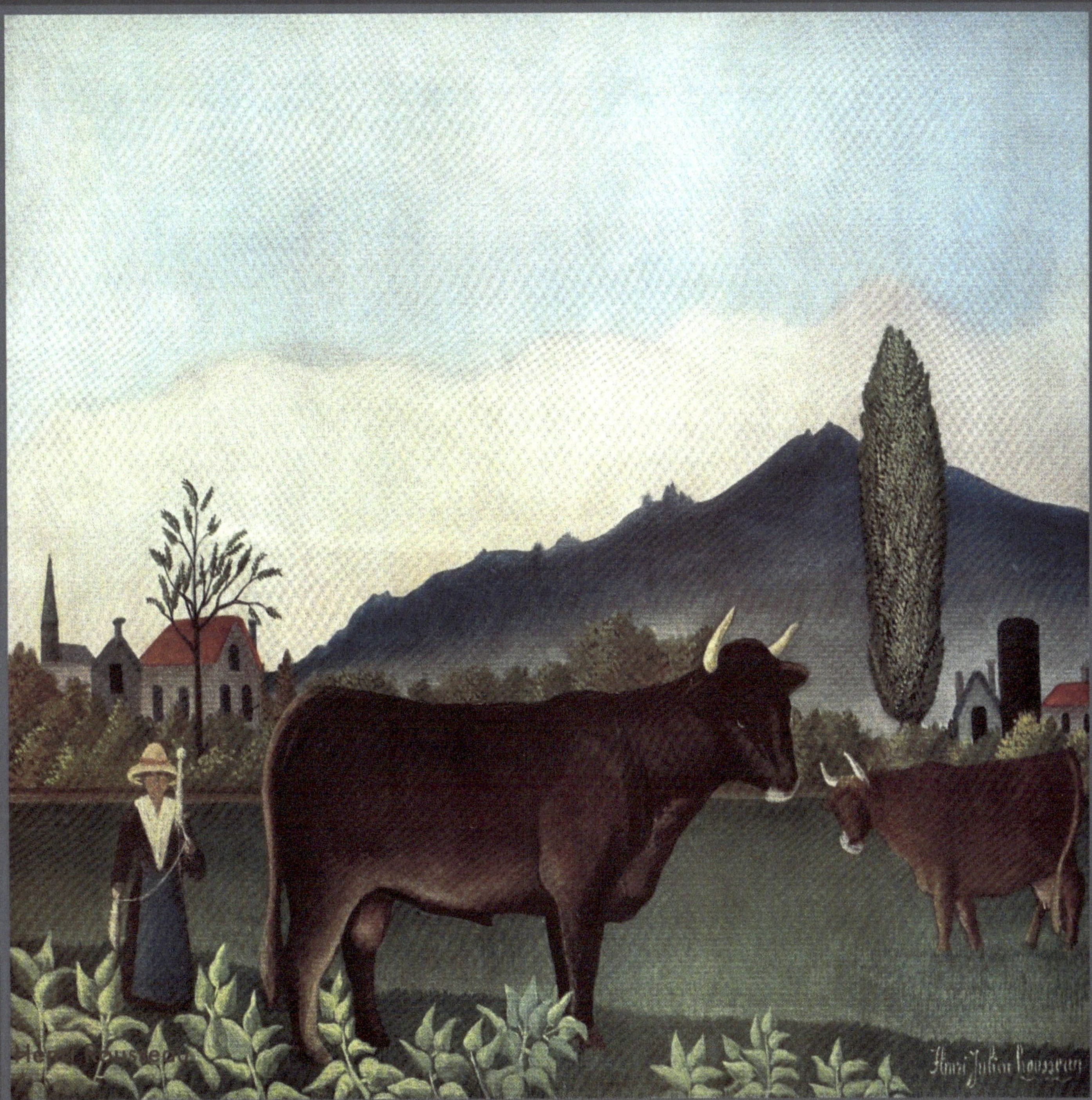
Henri Julien Rousseau

If I freely may discover
What should please me in my lover,
I would have her fair and witty.
Savoring more of court than city;
A little proud, but full of pity;
Light and humorous in her toying,
Oft building hopes, and soon destroying.
Long, but sweet in the enjoying;
Neither too easy nor to hard;
All extremes I would have barr'd.

—Ben Jonson

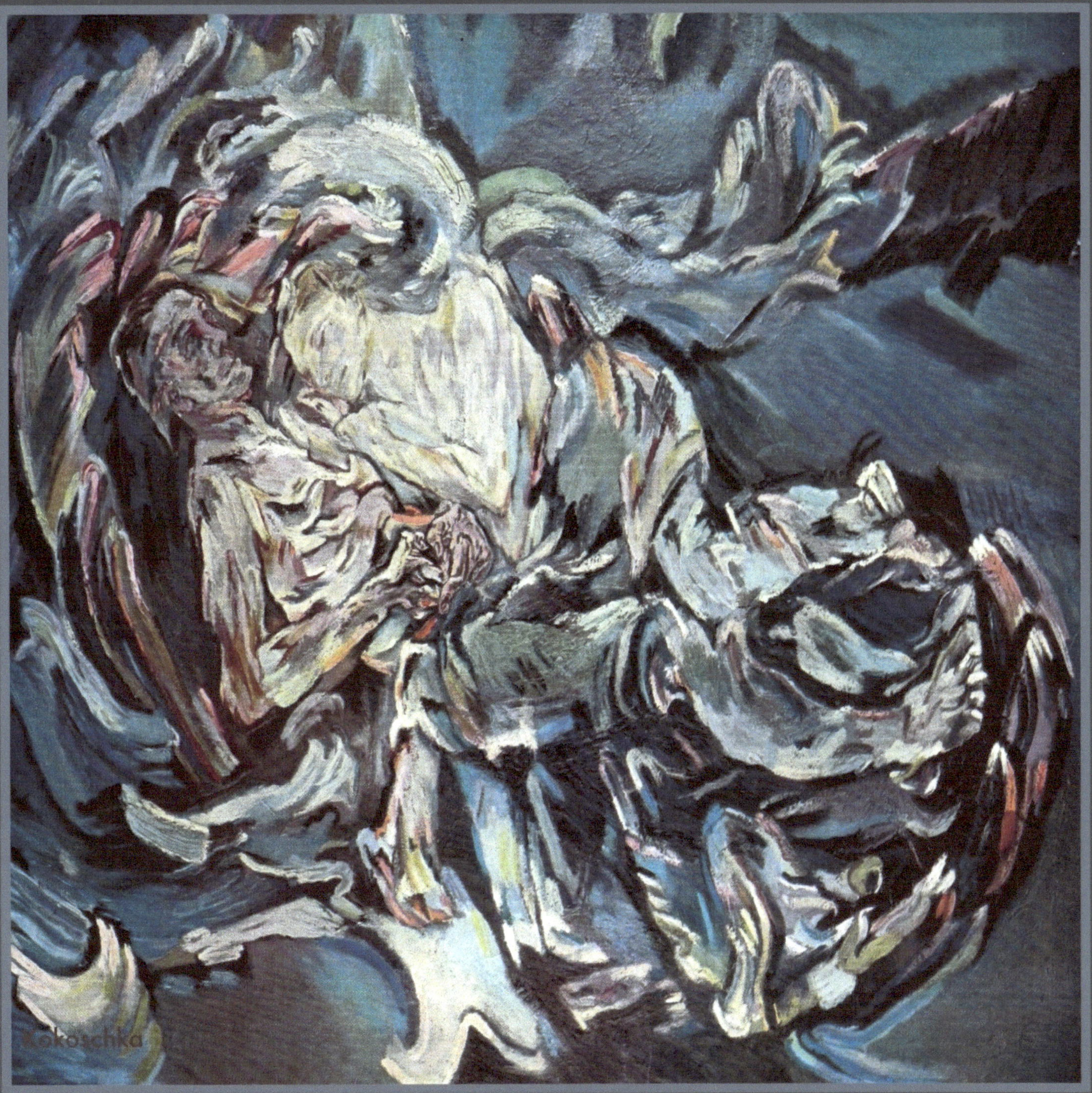

But just in proportion as we are not contented with our sphere, nor satisfied with ourselves, do we reach out longingly to a better sphere and a worthier course of life; and therefore it is that, to so many of us, the end of an old year brings a sense of relief, in that its shortcomings and failures are now to be left behind, while the approach of a new year suggests a hope of something different and better beyond, in the path we are treading.

— Sunday School Times

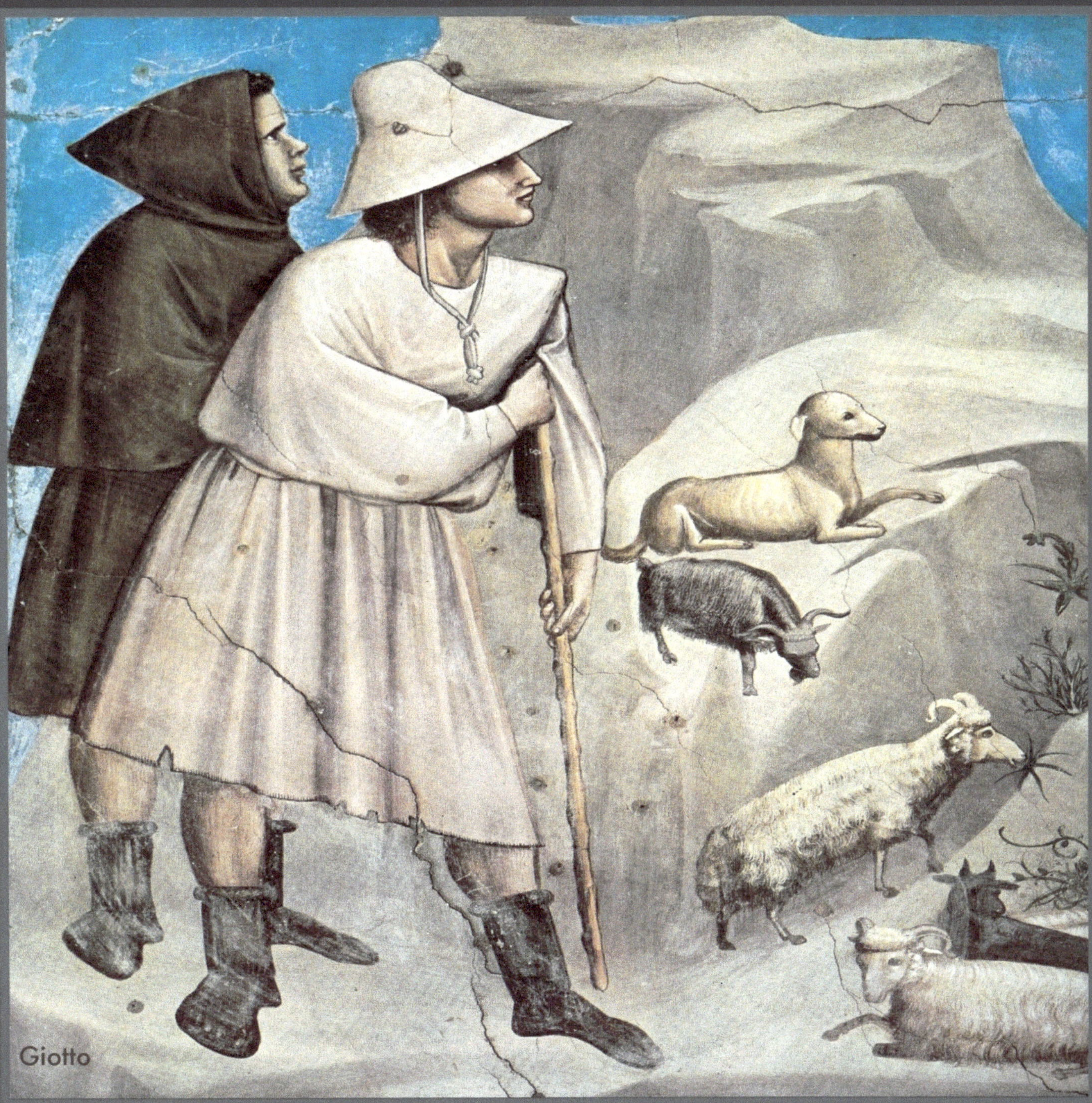

Giotto

Isoken

Gallery Notes

www.ingramcontent.com/pod-product-compliance
Lightning Source LLC
LaVergne TN
LVHW070140110826
845147LV00002B/295